The Still Lifes of Photographer
Marco Leonardi: A Room of One's Own

Suzanne Fredericq and Marília Giannini

ISBN: 978-0-9825704-3-2

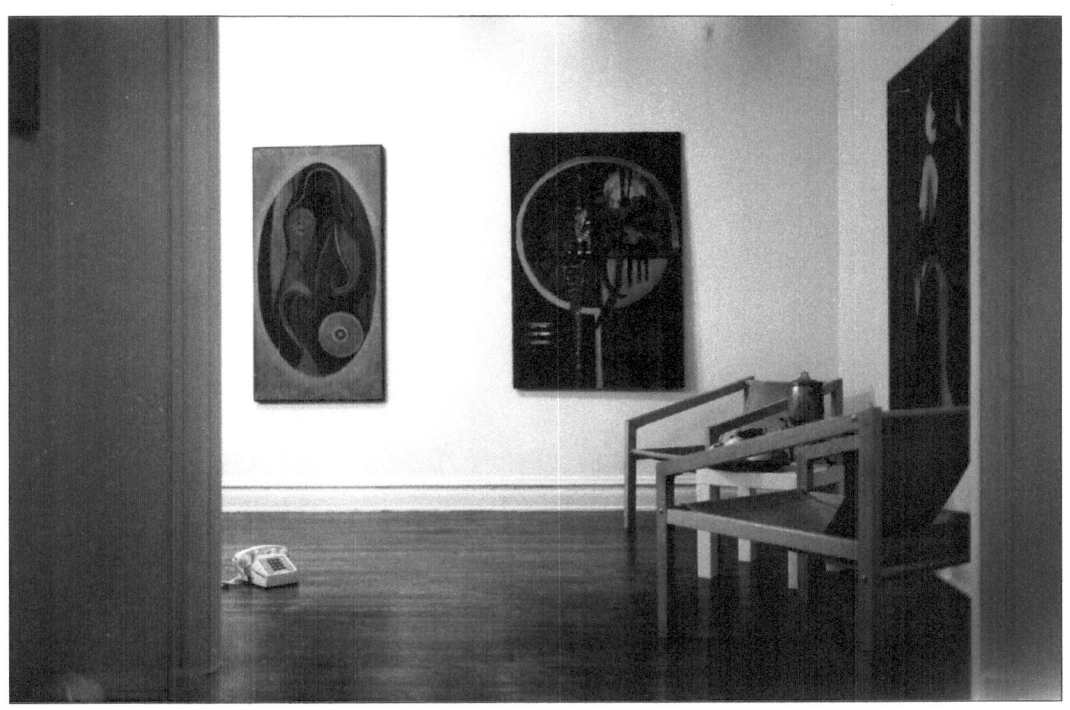

"When music is far enough away
the eyelid does not often move

and objects are still as lavender
without breath or distant rejoinder."

Frank O'Hara (from 'A Quiet Poem')

Foreword

Marco Leonardi was born in Sanremo on the Italian Riviera in 1933, a city where he spent his youth in the years preceding and during World War II. As a teenager in the 1940's he left home and spent over 25 years traveling and living in many countries, including several years in the merchant marine. Traveling made him more visually attuned, which led him to photography.

Leonardi came to the United Stated in the early 1960's, lived in New York City for several years, and traveled throughout the country. From the mid-1970's until his death from complications of leukemia in 1990, he had made Washington D.C. his home.

Marco Leonardi shared his apartment with his close friend, the visual artist Eugene James Martin, from the late 1970's until 1988. Martin taught him how to look at art and how to focus on photography.

This compilation includes 59 black and white, and color photographs of still-life tableaux captured by Marco Leonardi in his Washington D.C. apartment. The original photographs and Ektachrome and Kodachrome slides were taken between 1981 and 1988 and converted to digital files for use in this publication.

Additional photographs by Marco Leonardi can be viewed at:

Fredericq S. & Giannini M. 2009. A Walk through the City: Photographer Marco Leonardi's Architectural Washington D.C. 145 pp., Estate of Eugene James Martin.

http://youtube.com/moonlightnoir

http://www.saatchi-gallery.co.uk/yourgallery/artist_profile/artpage/40598.html

Suzanne Fredericq, Lafayette, Louisiana
Marília Giannini, São Paulo, Brasil
October 15, 2009

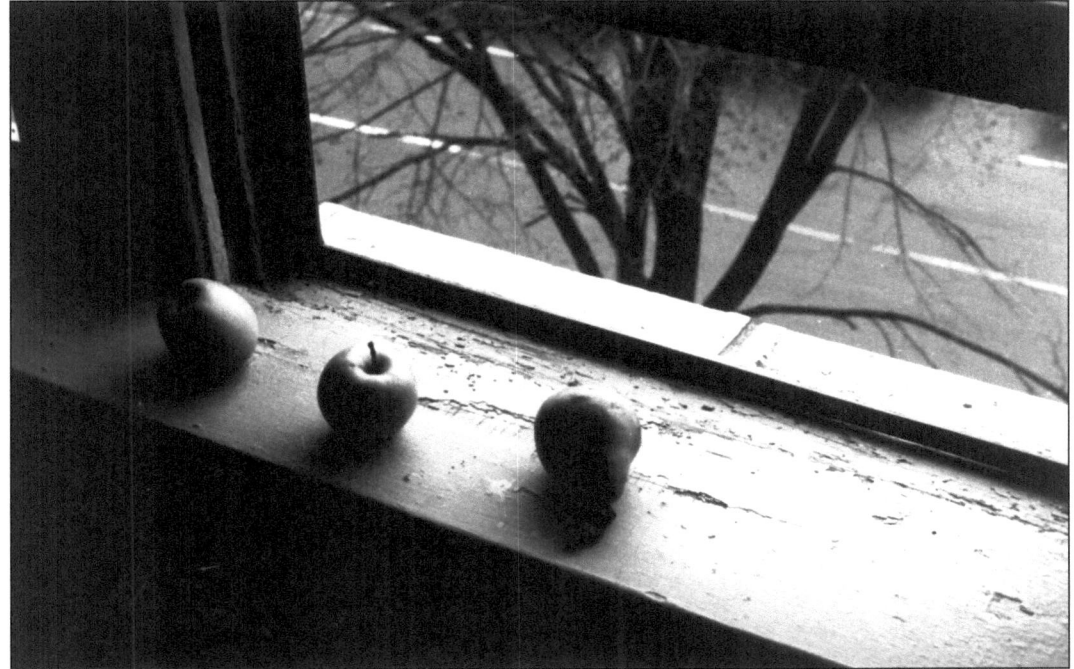

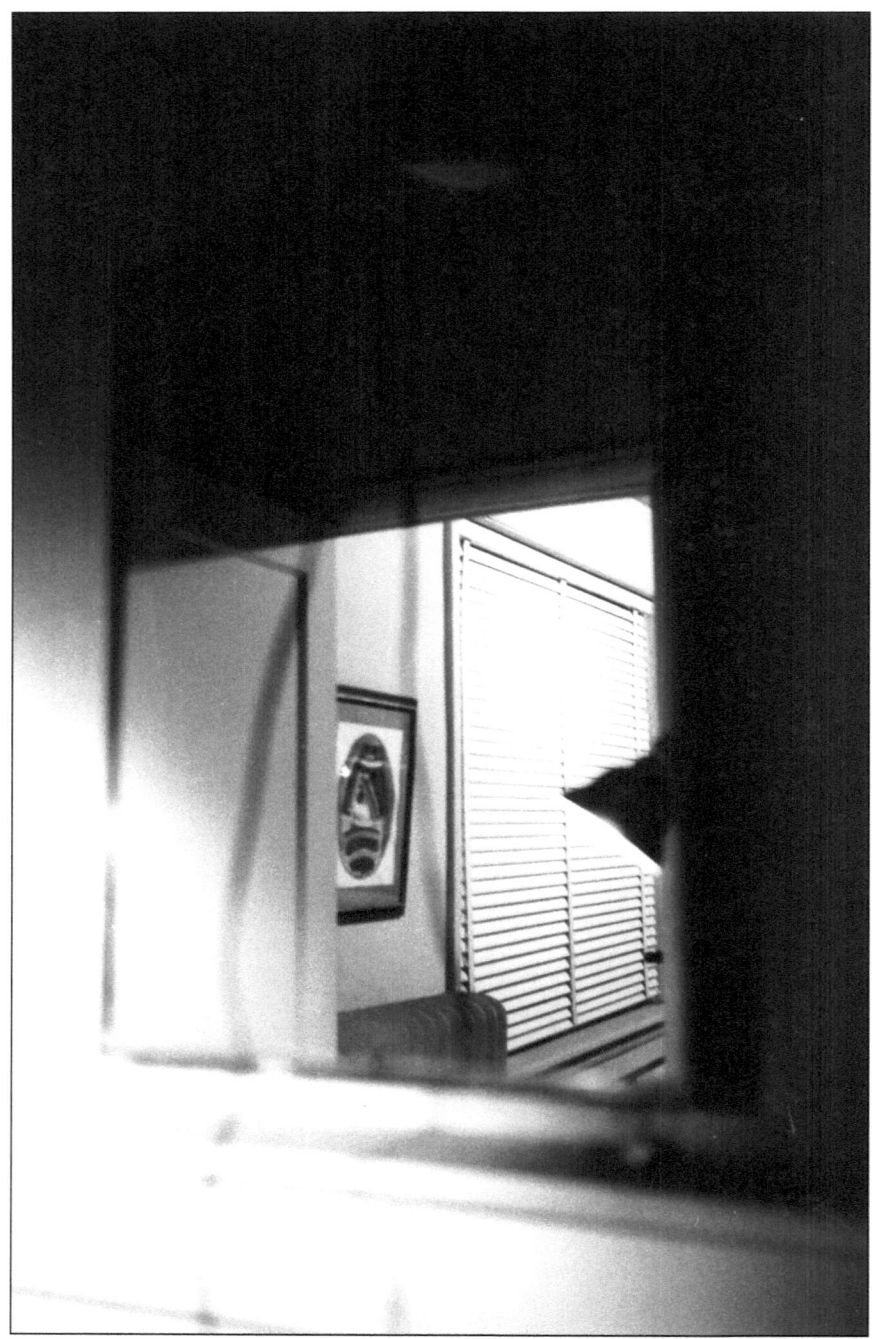

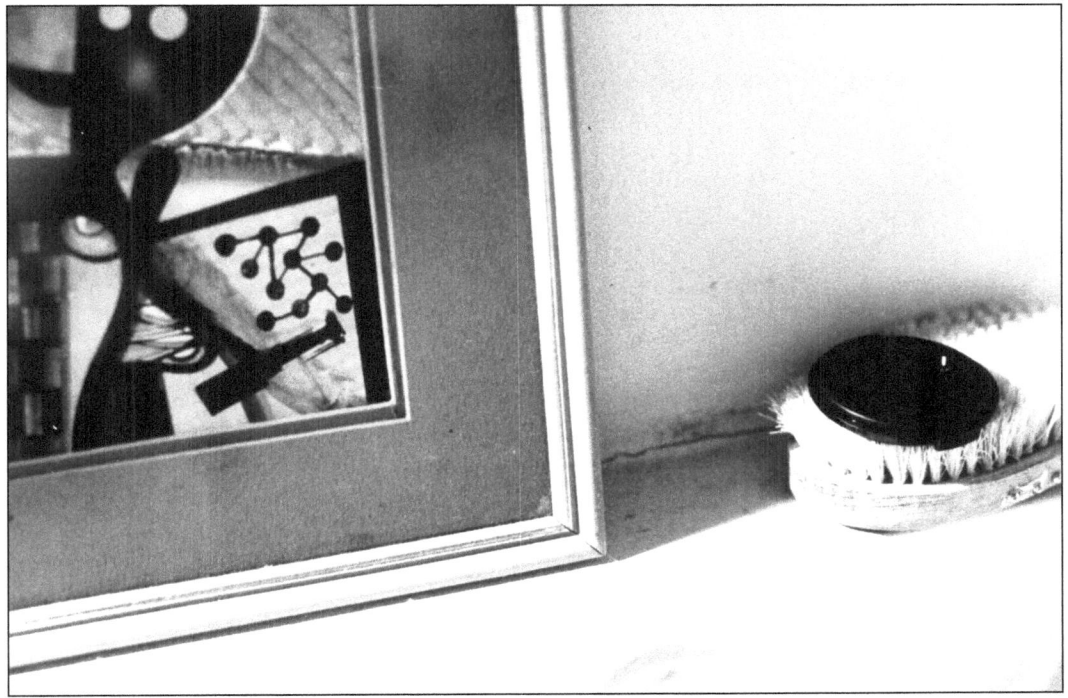

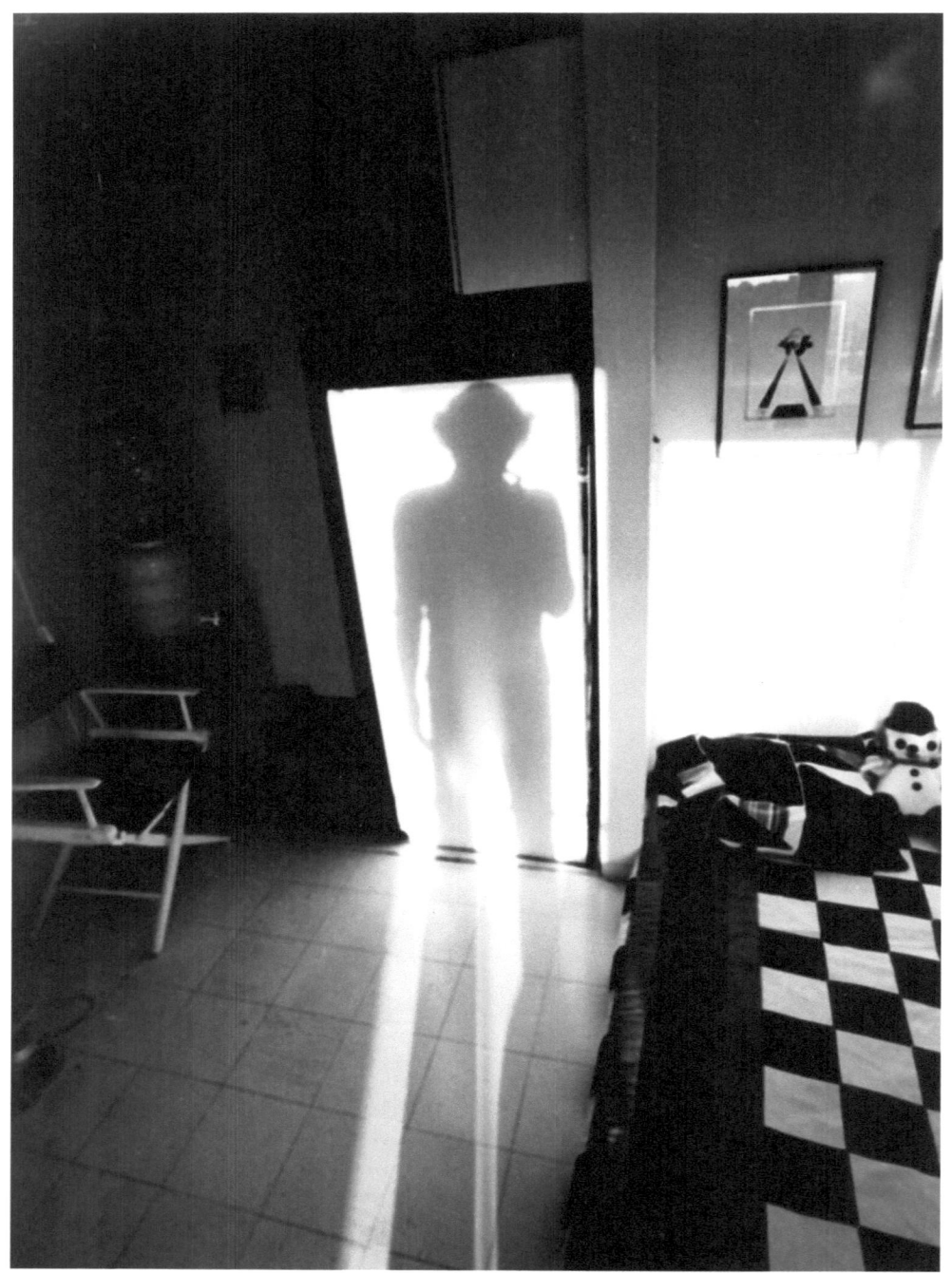

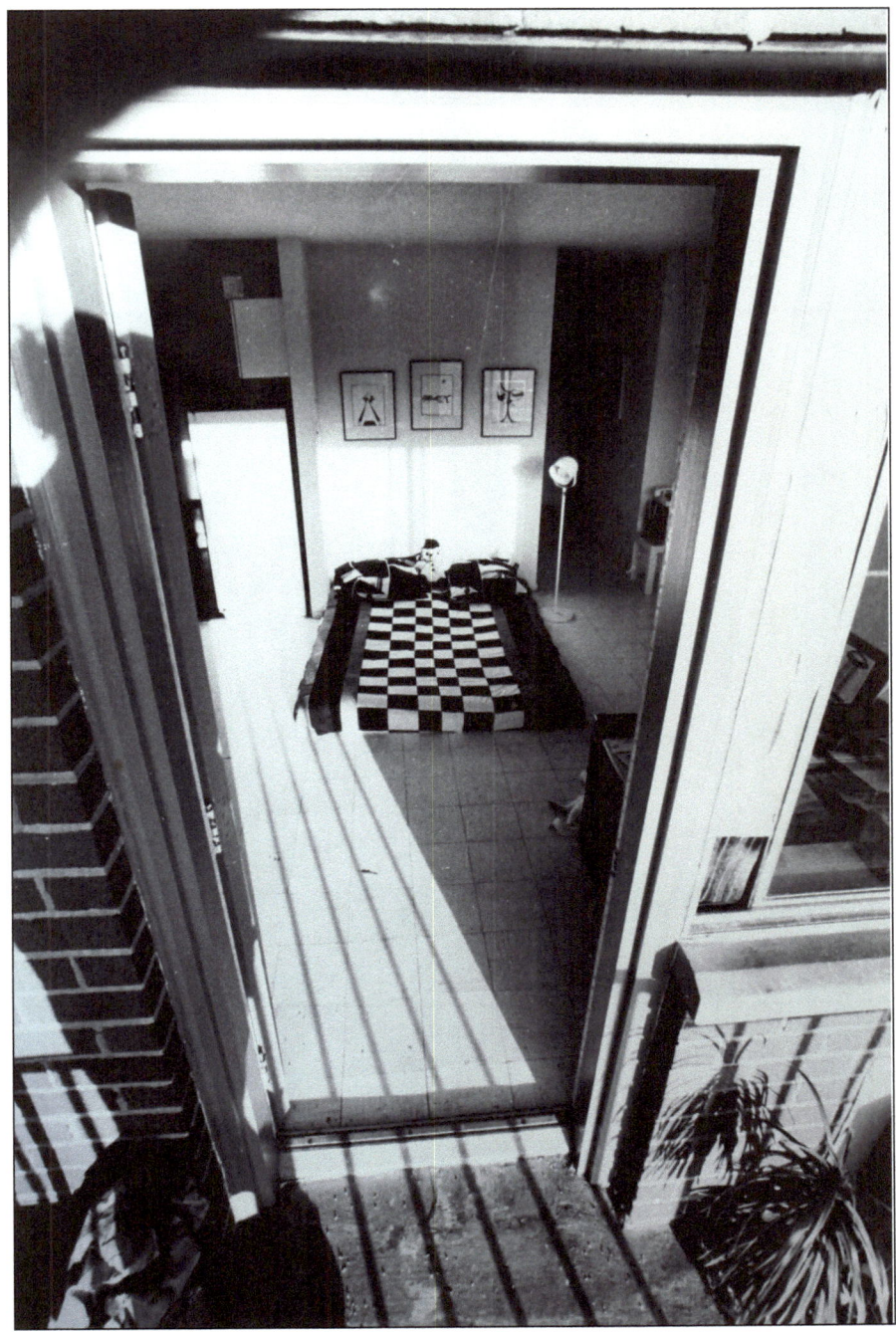

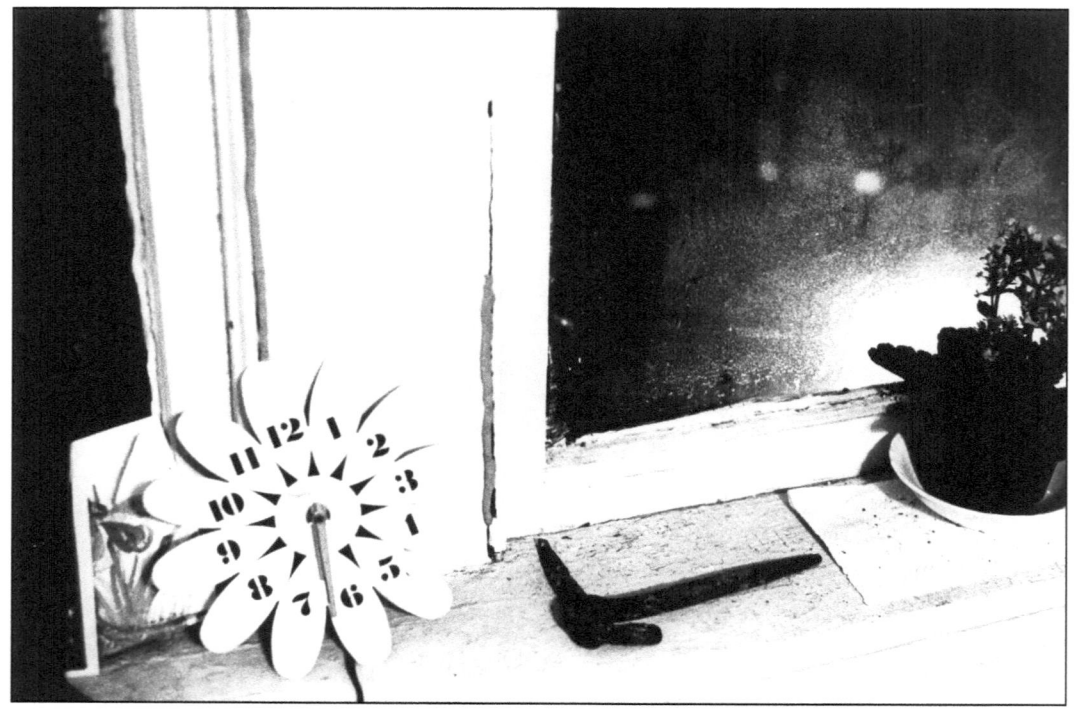

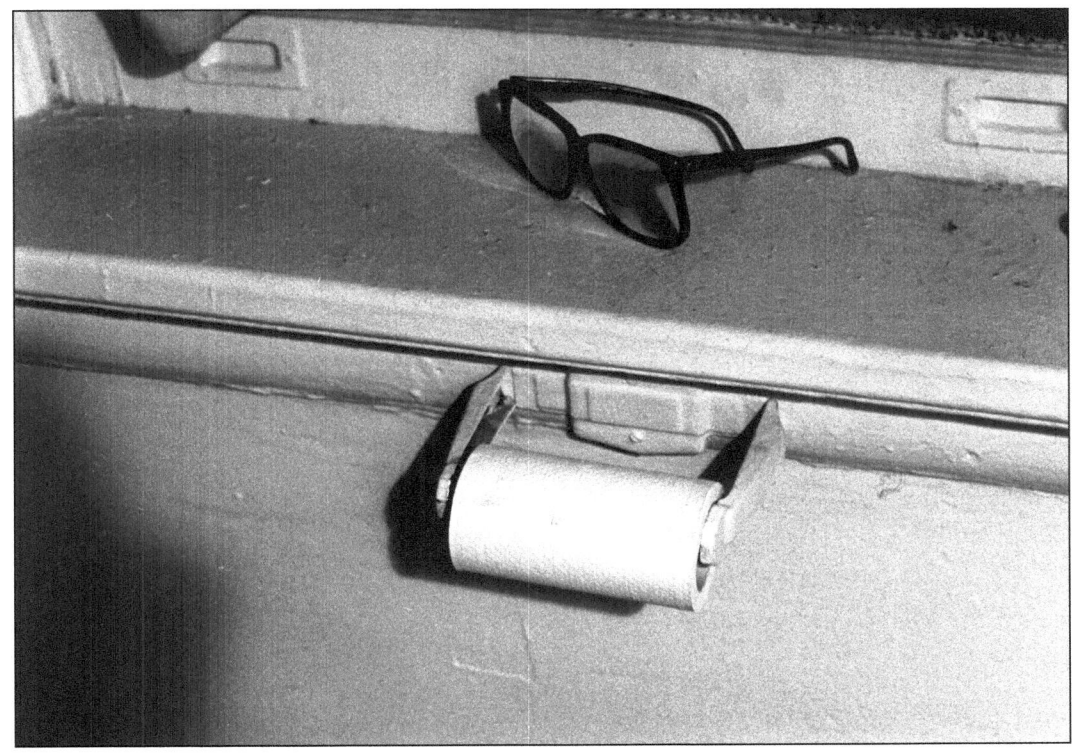

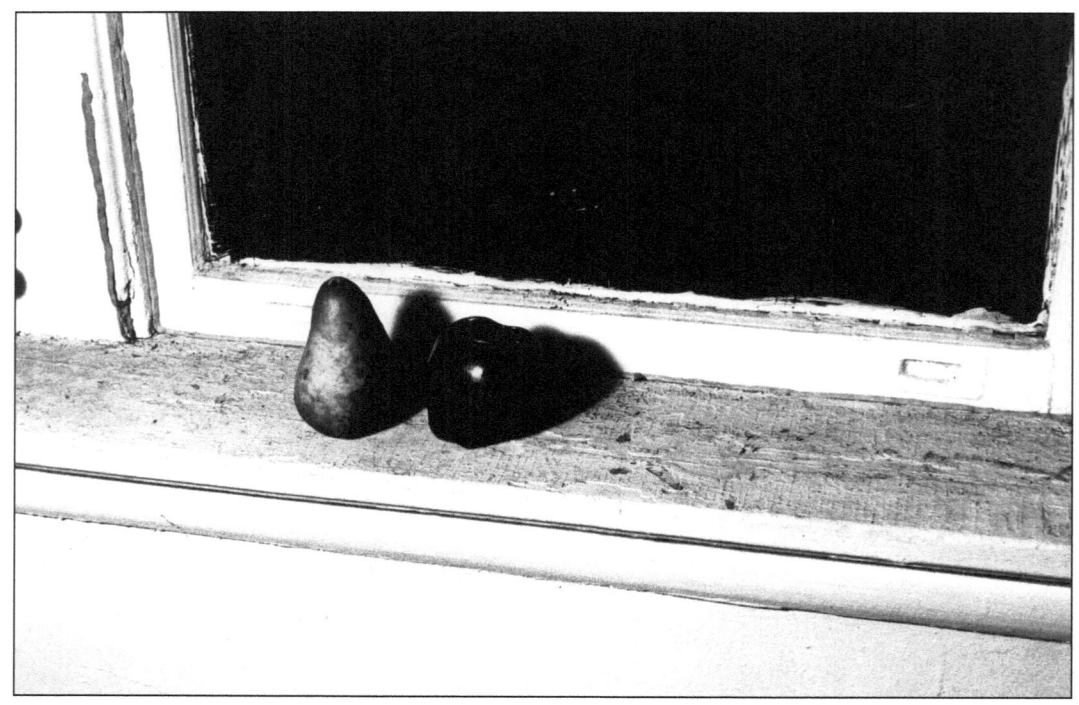

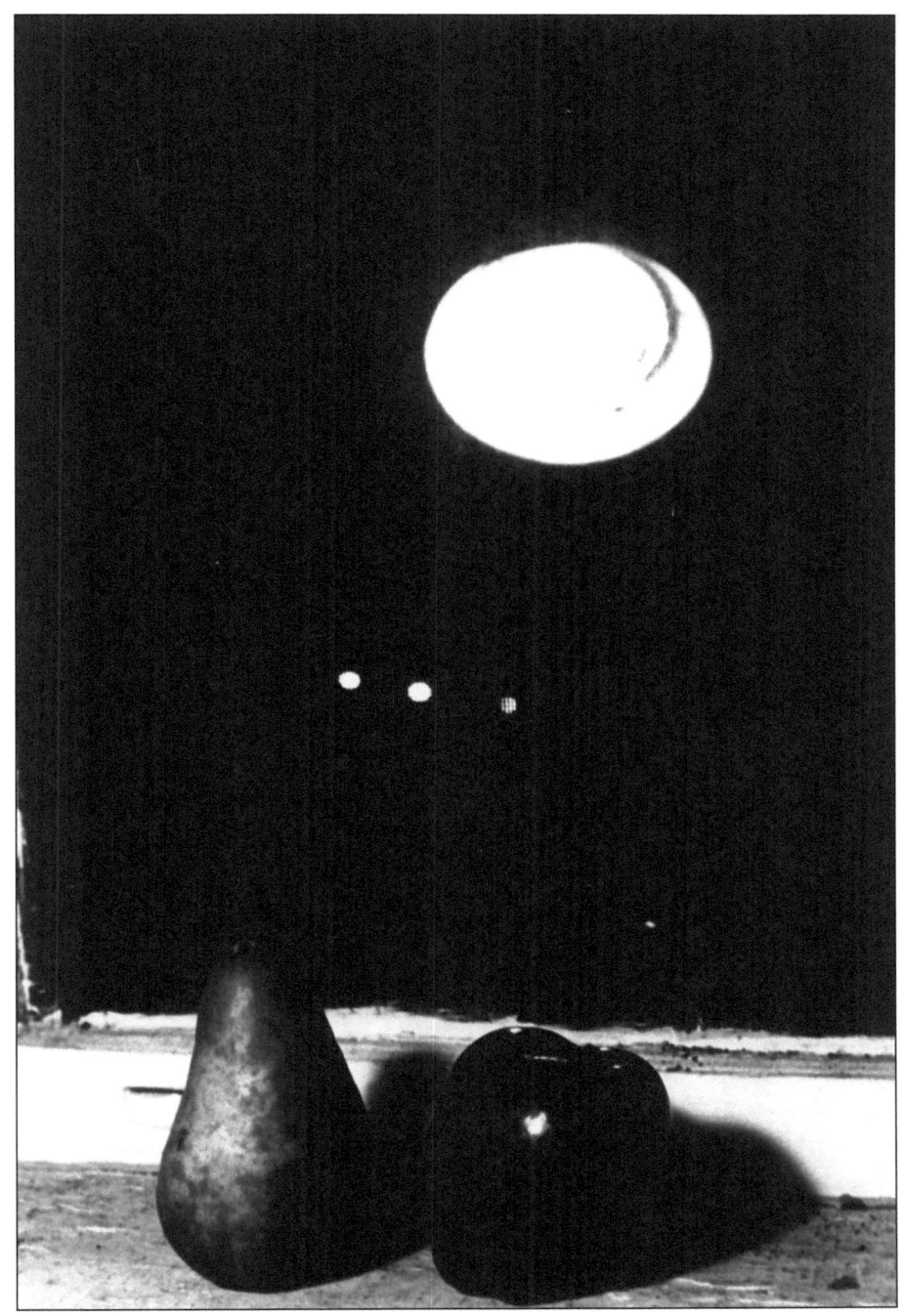

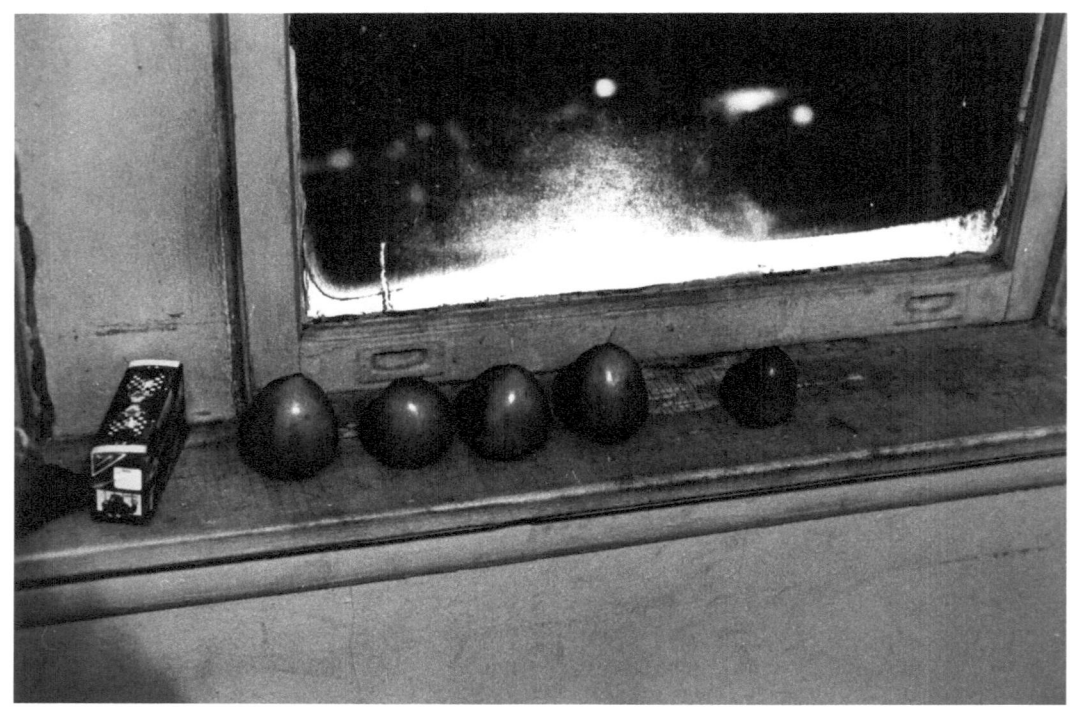

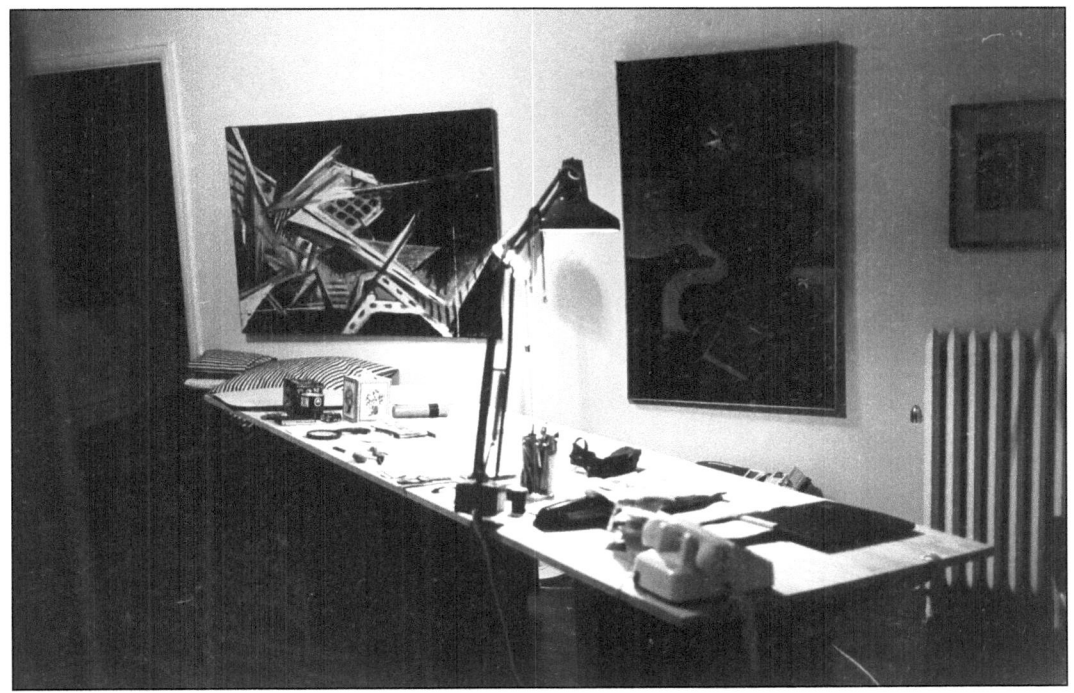

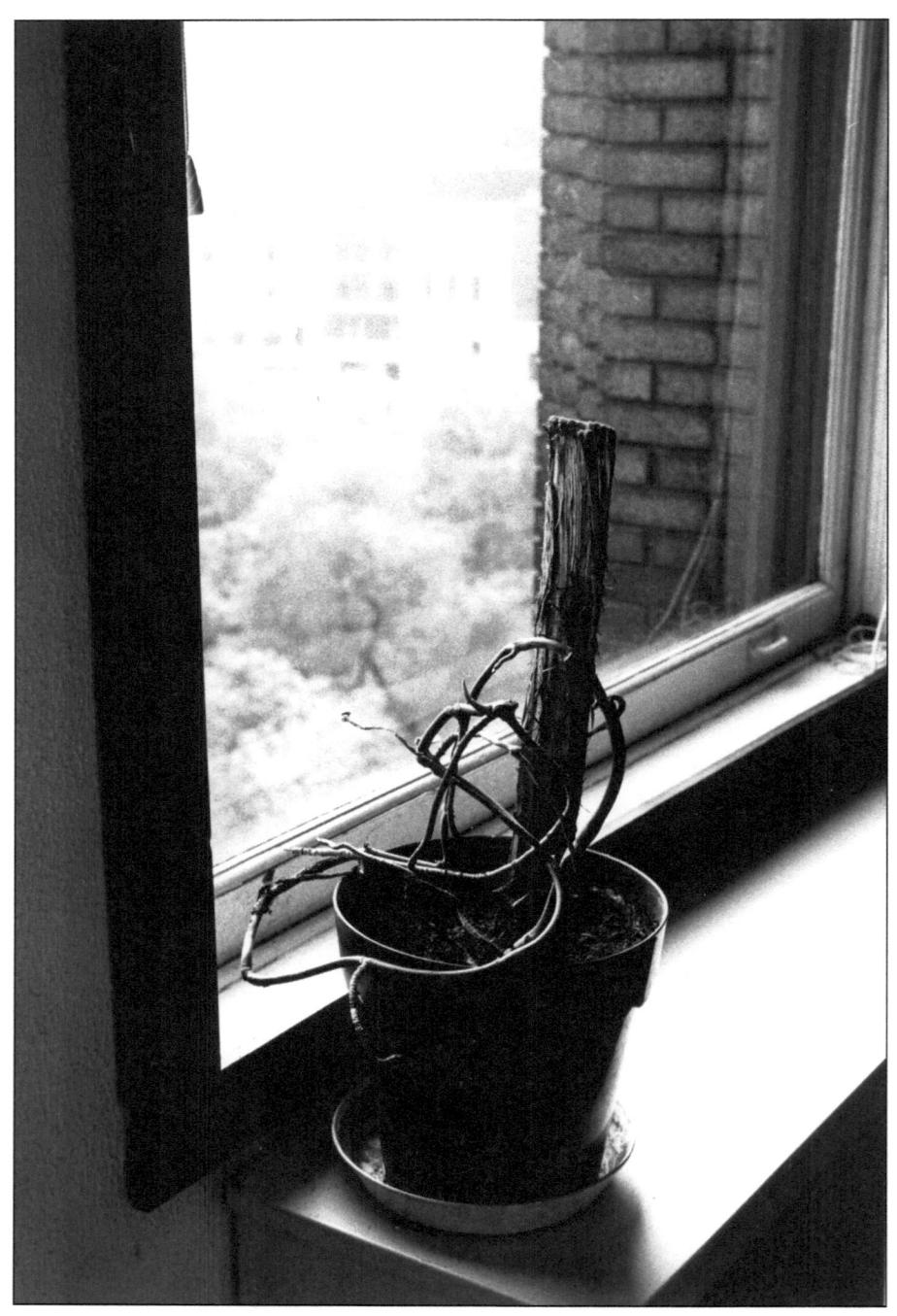

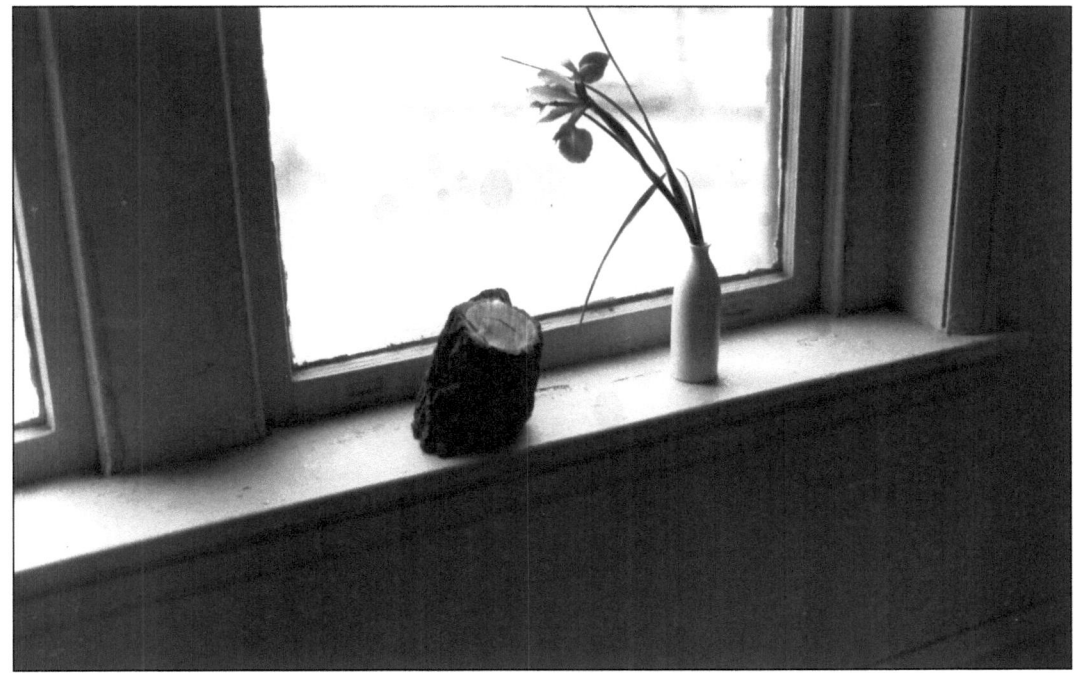

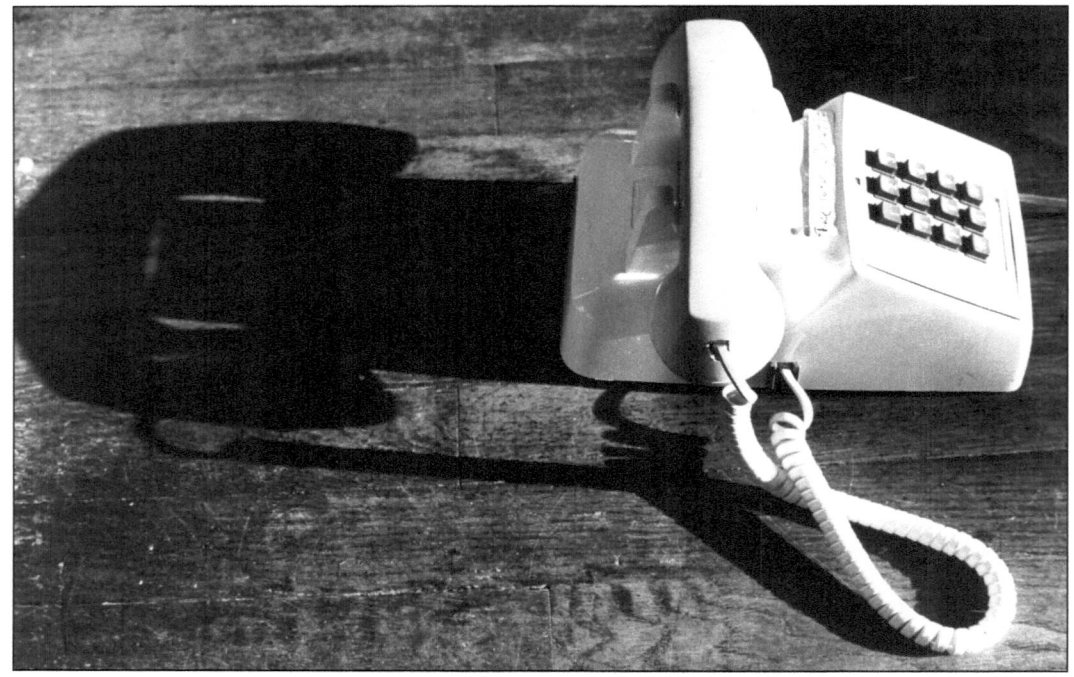

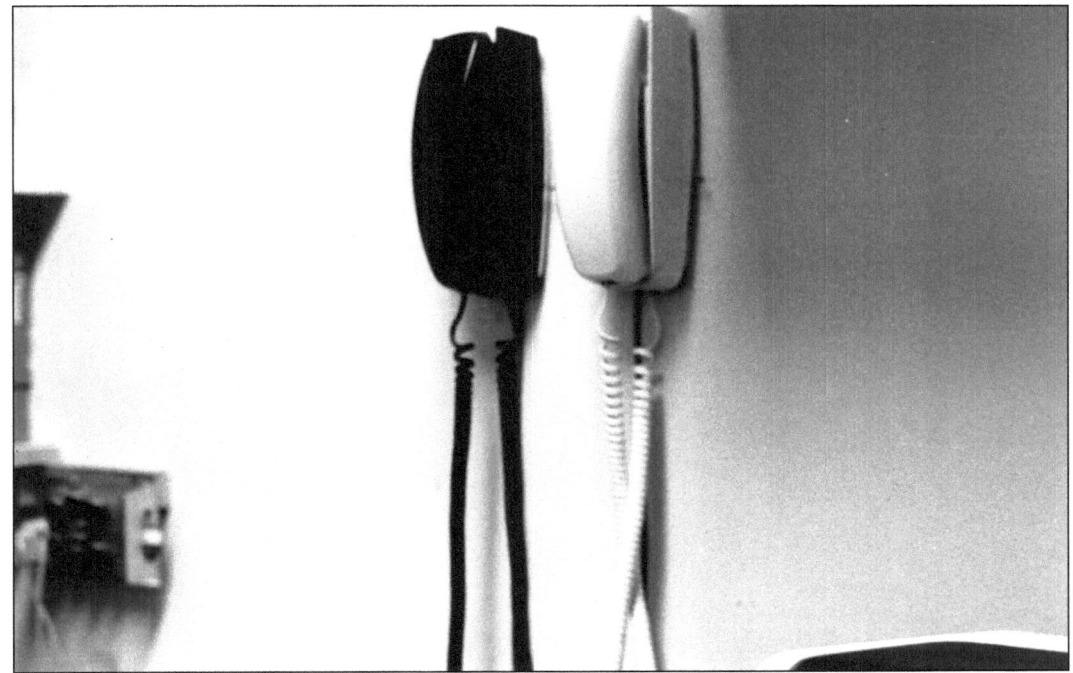

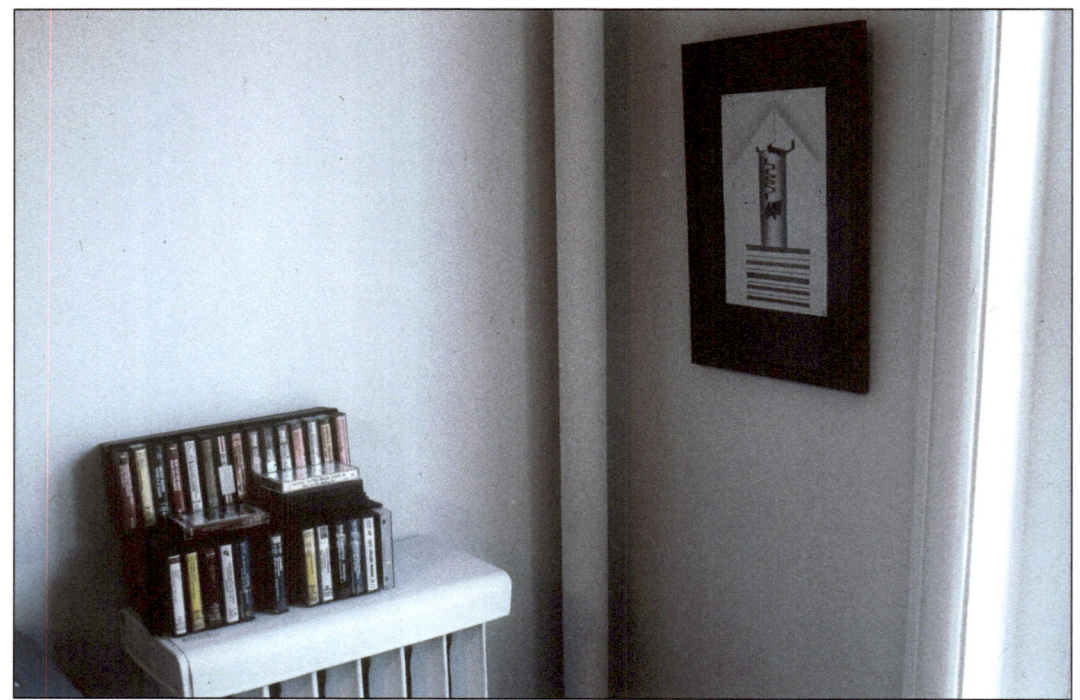

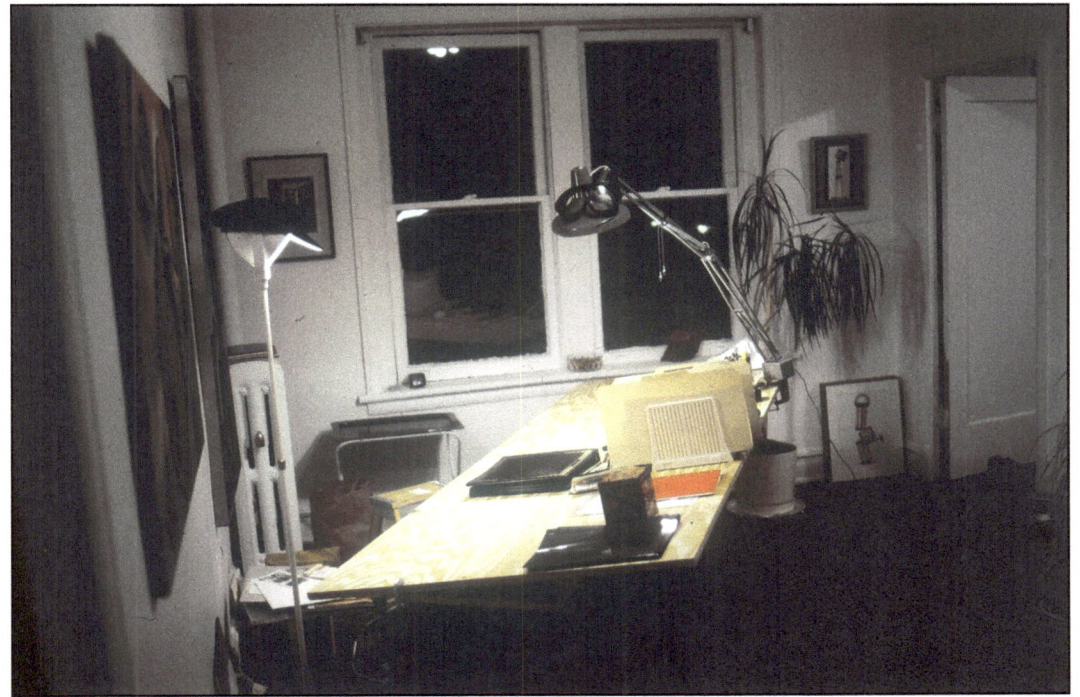

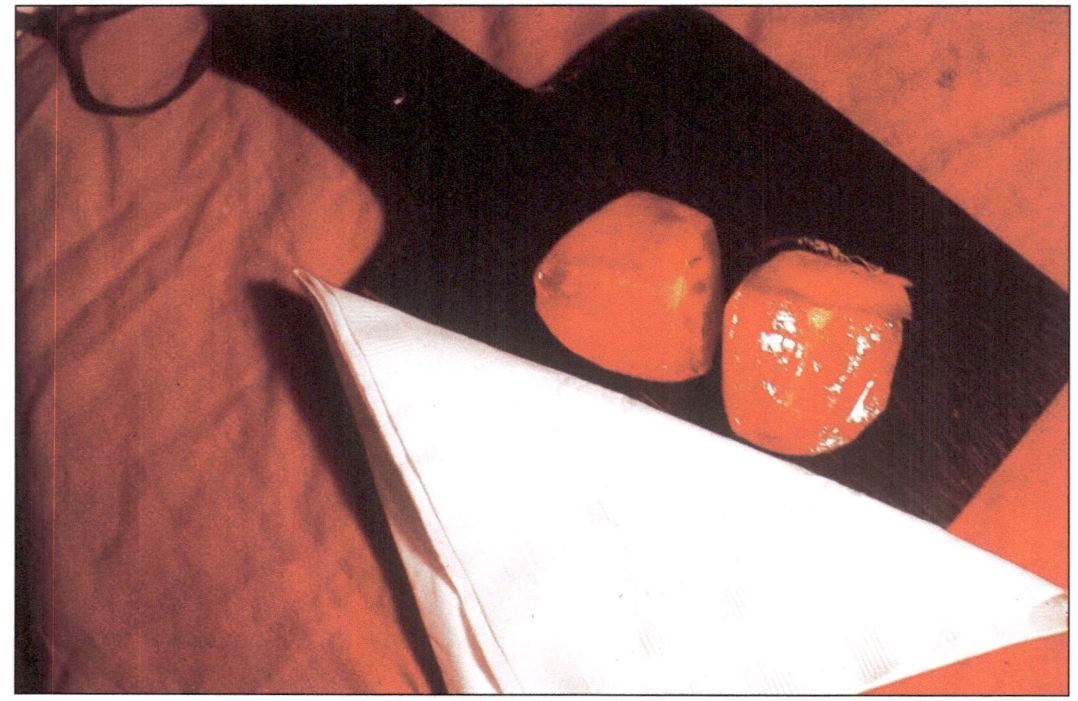

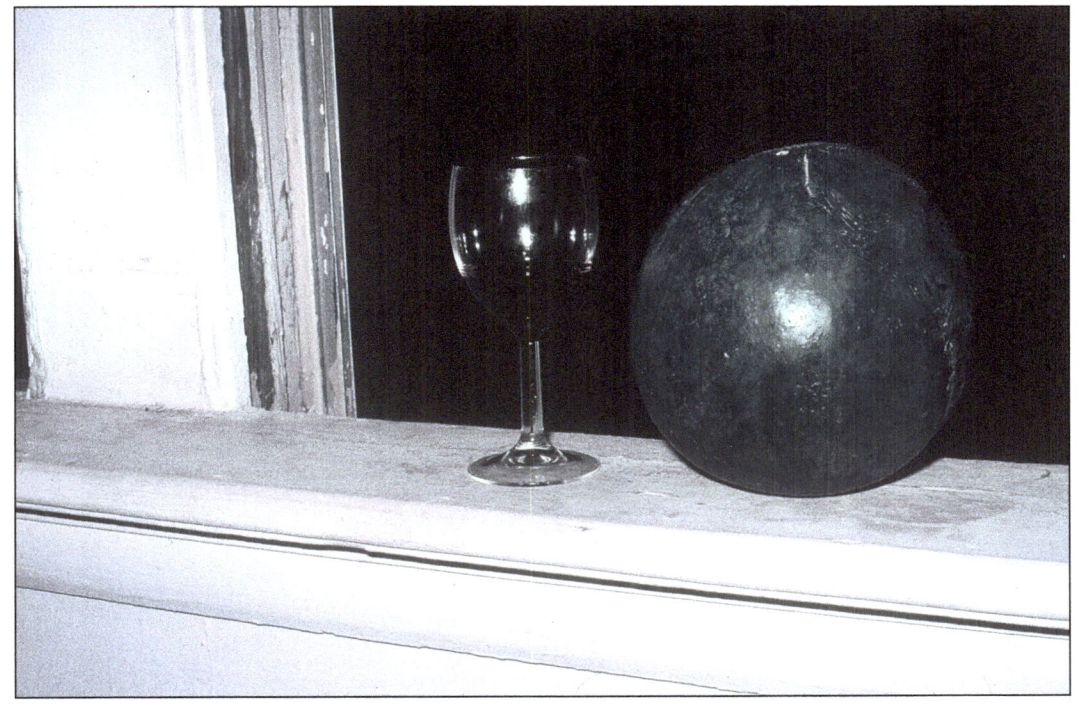

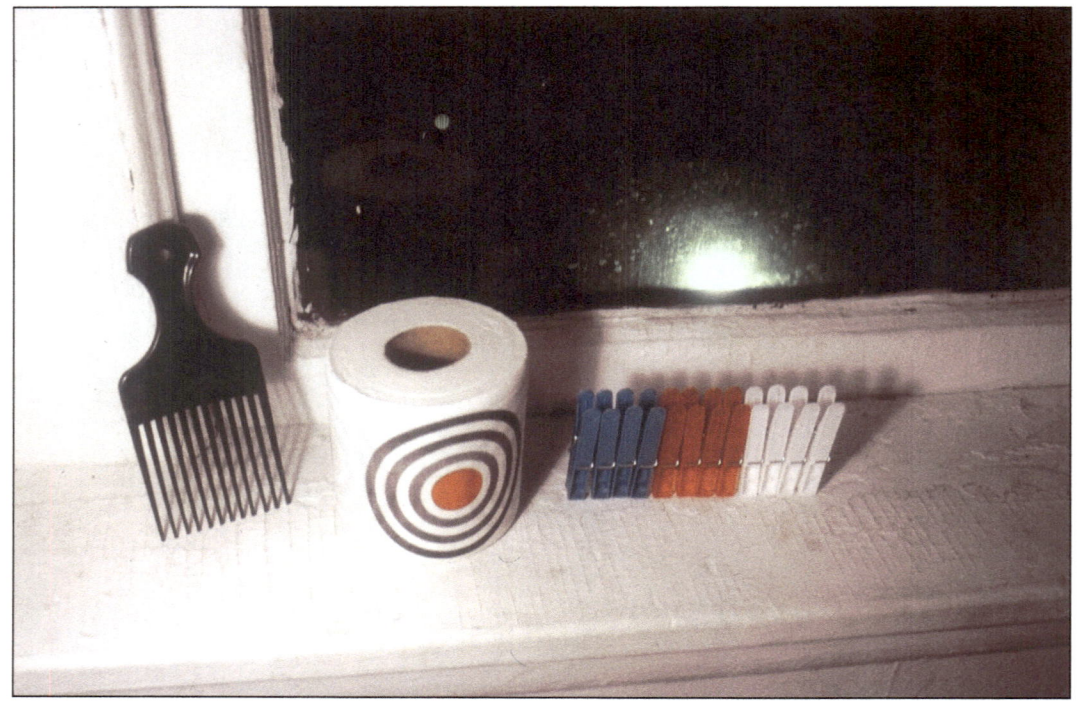

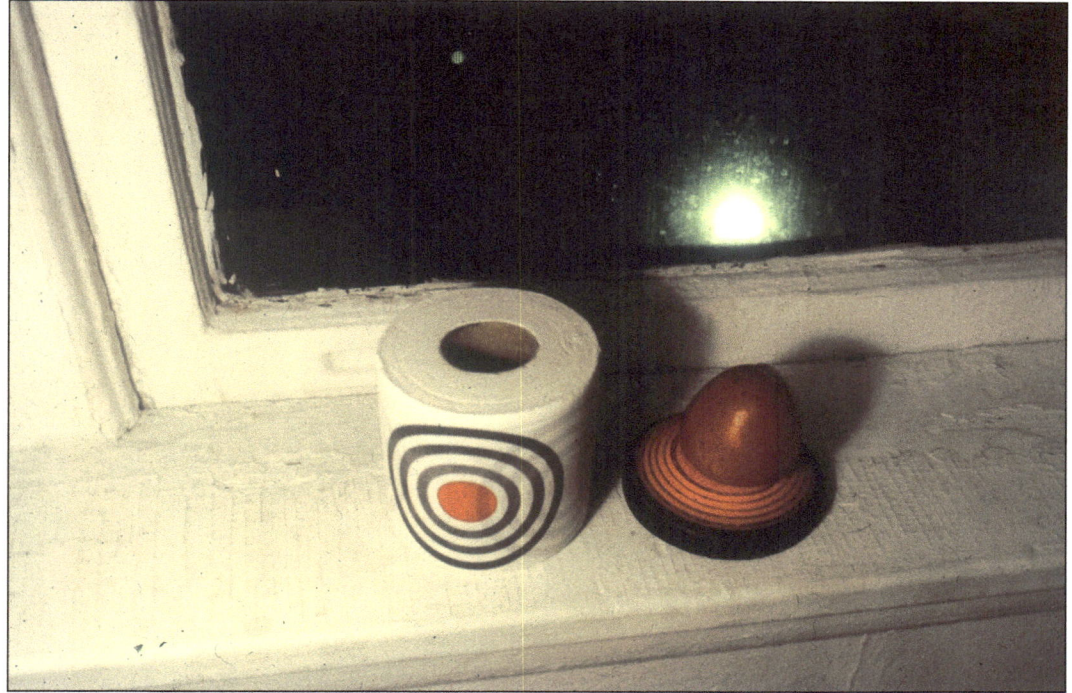

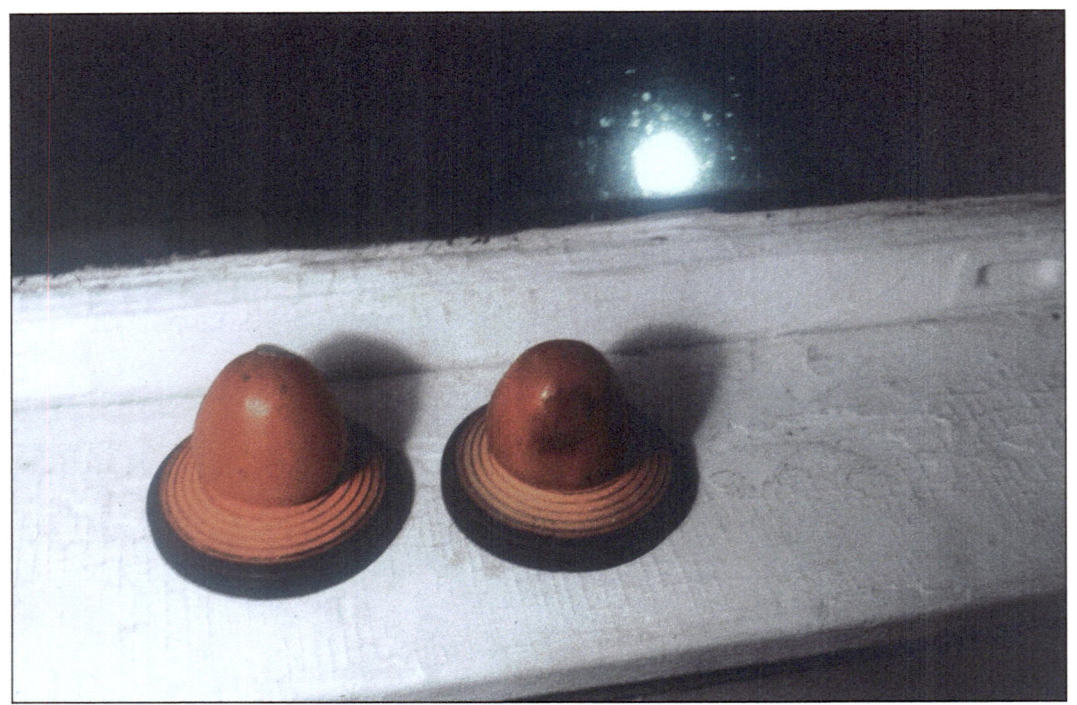

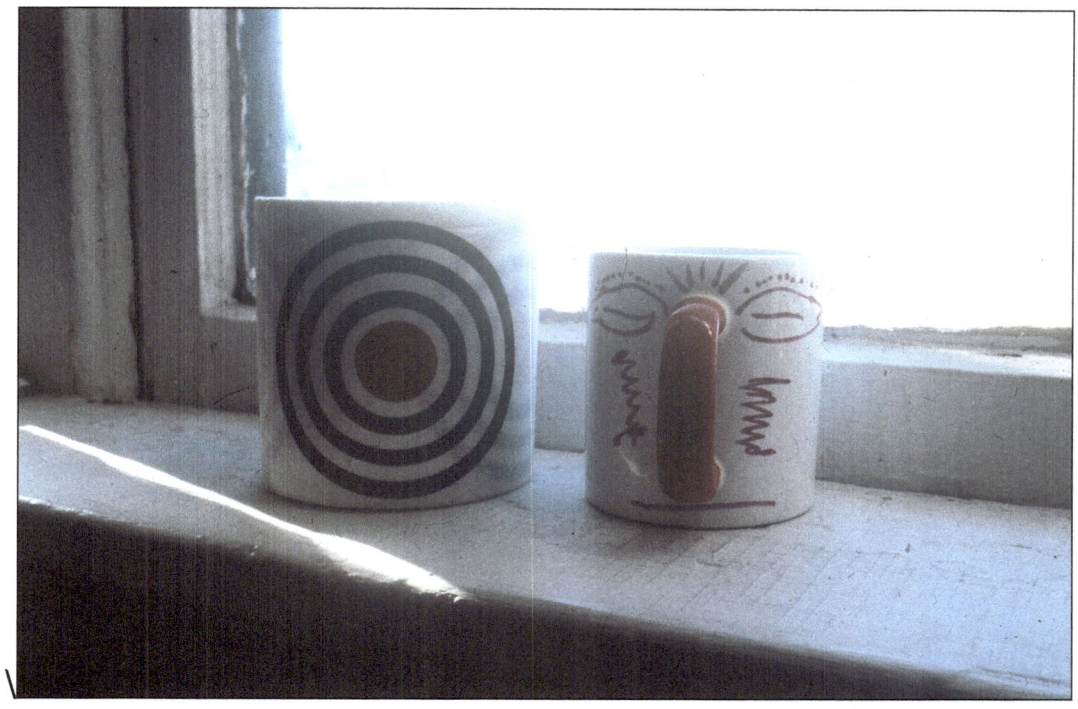

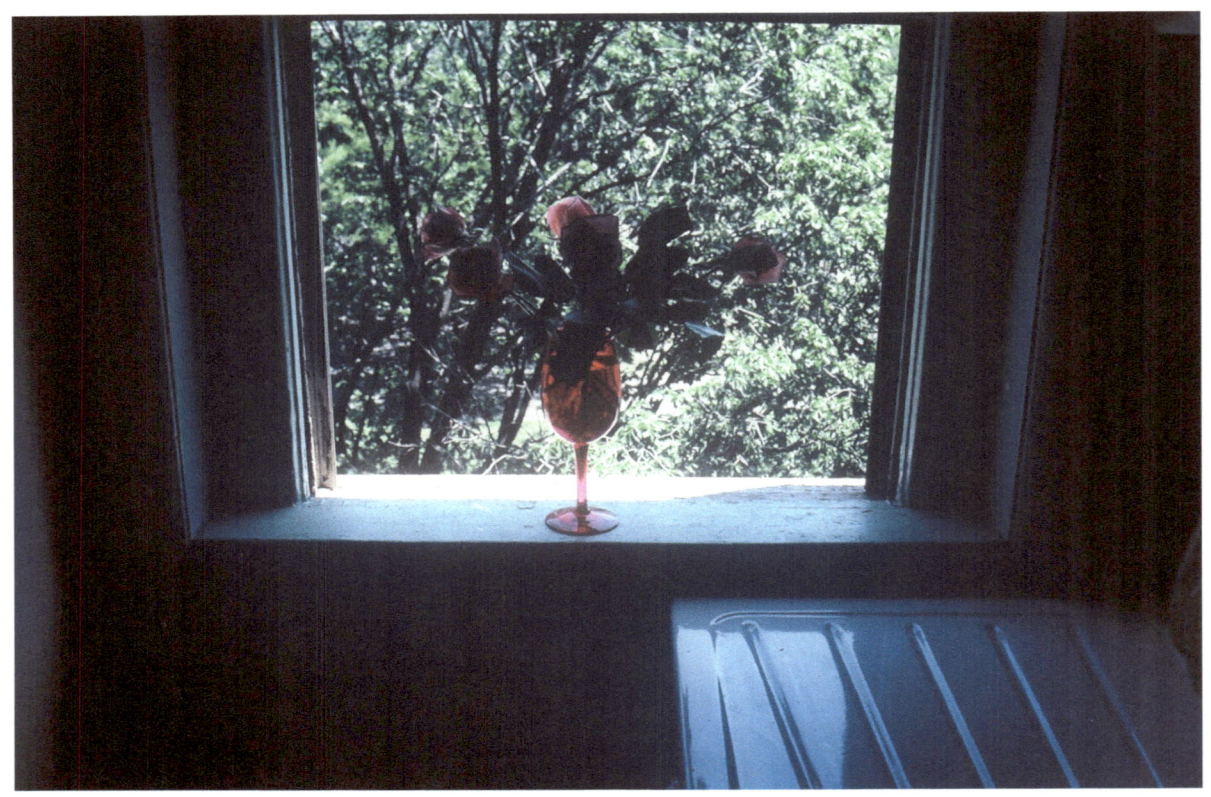

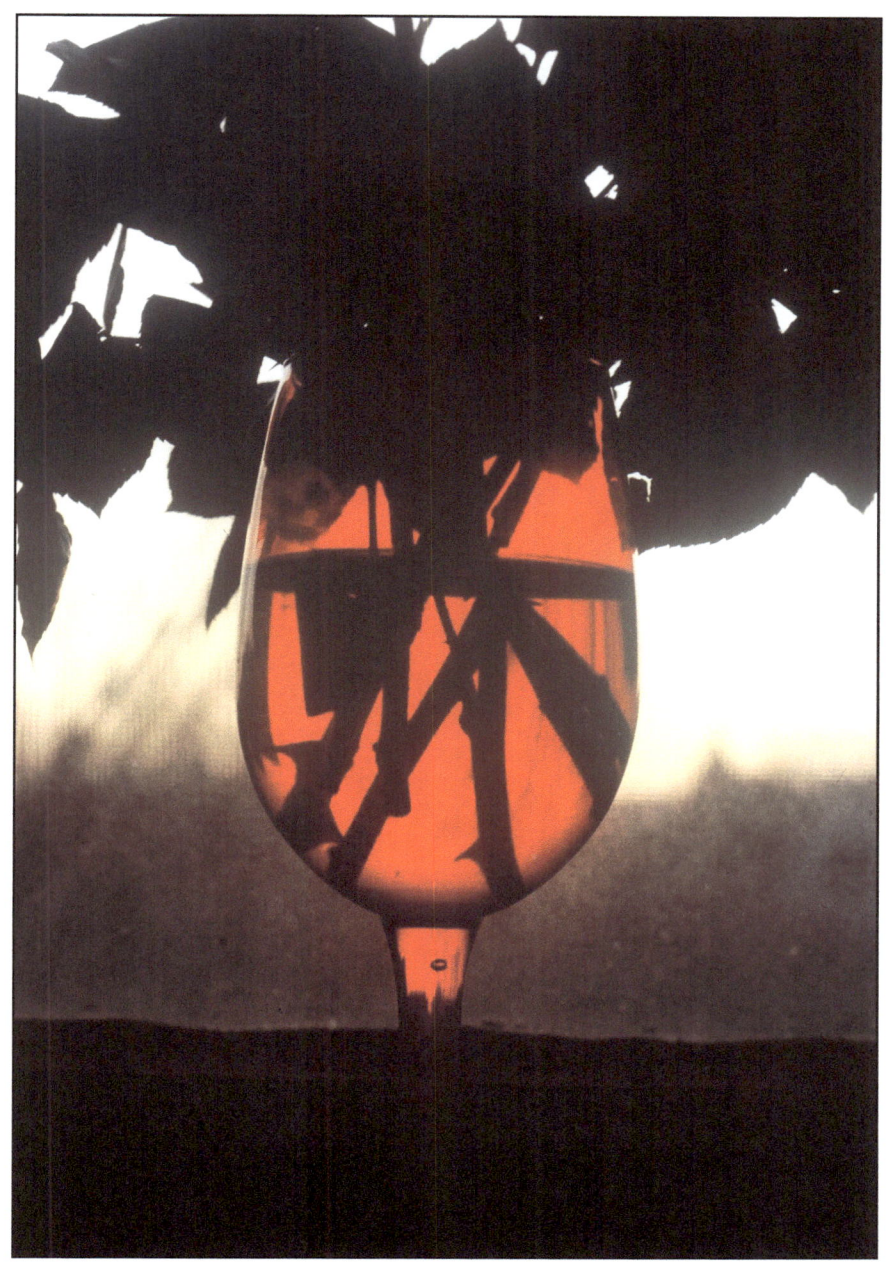

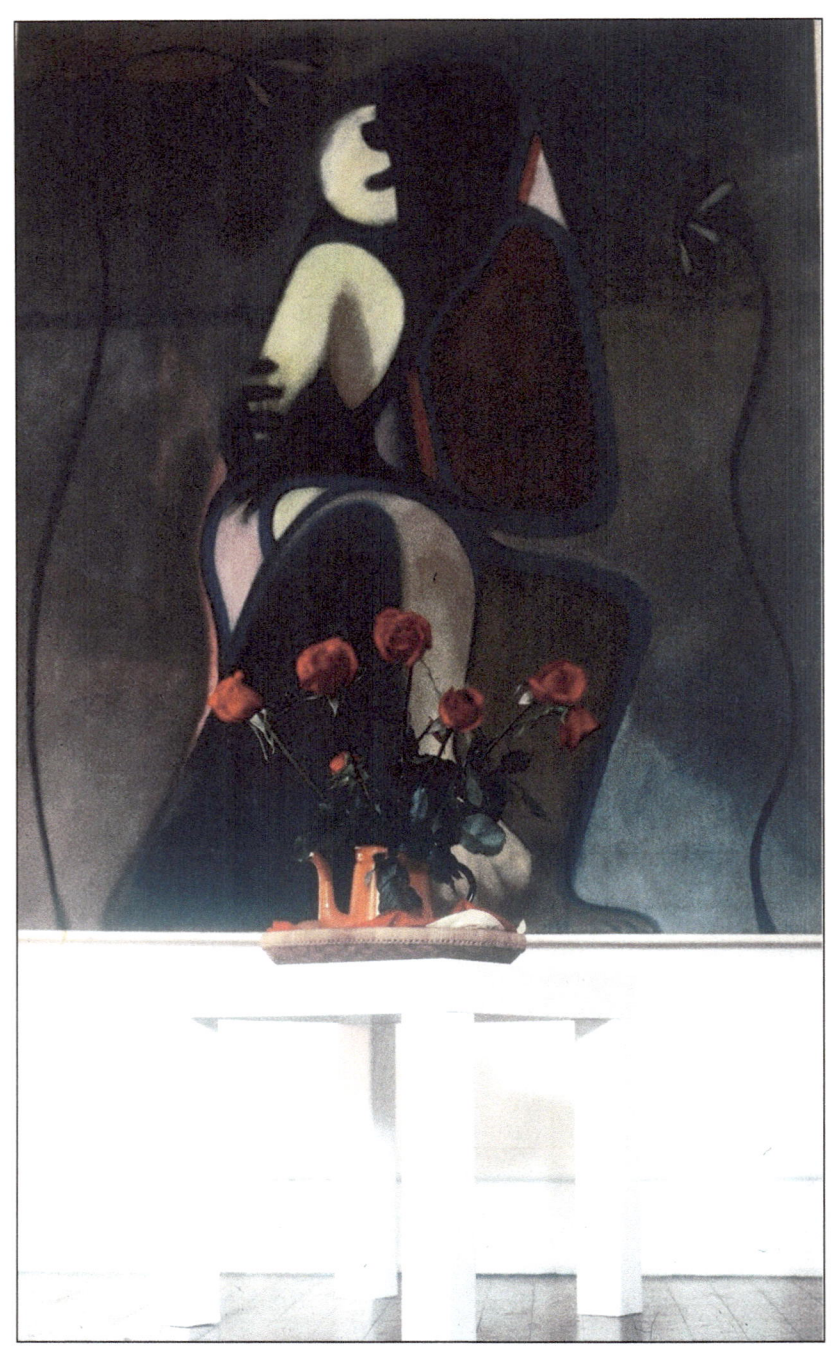

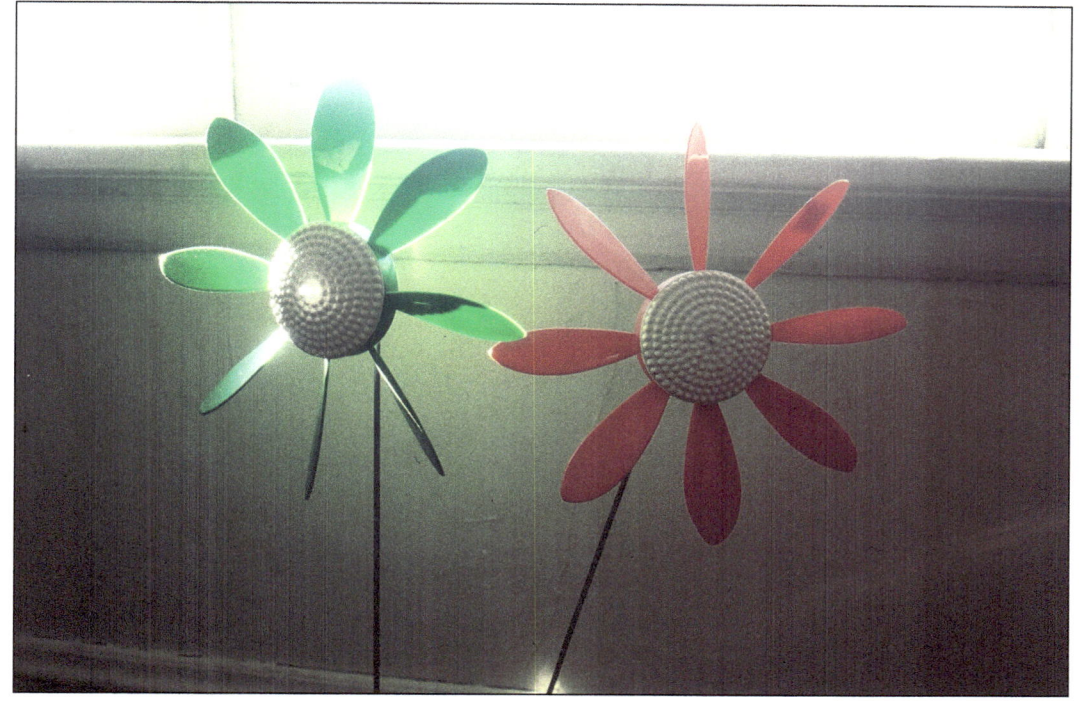

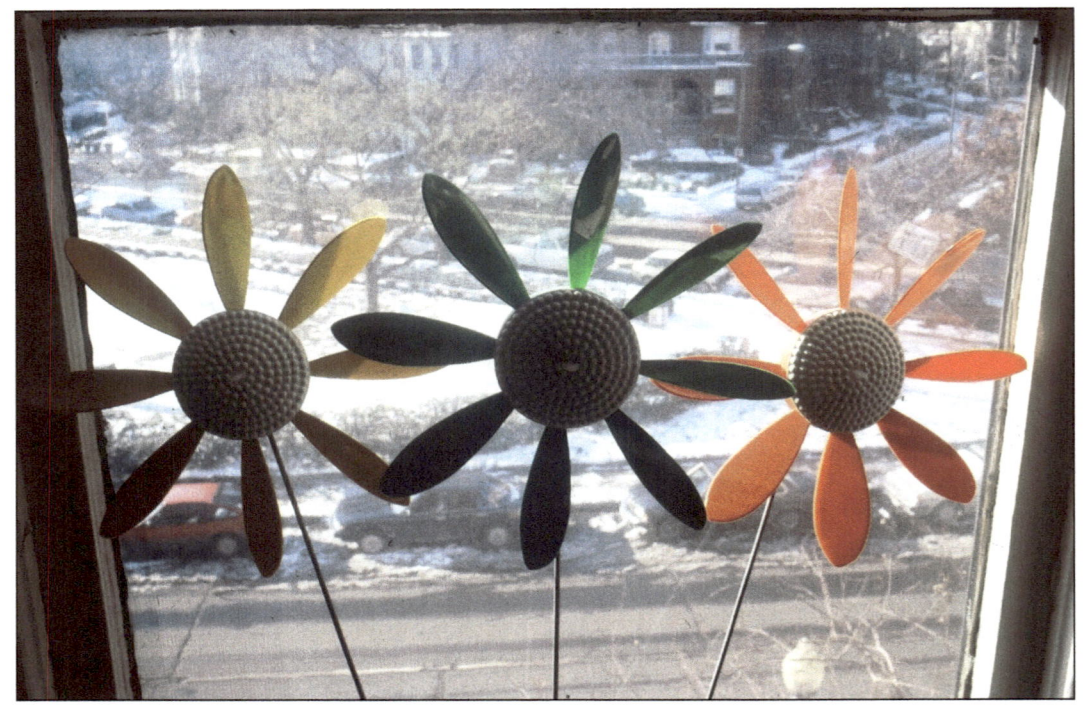

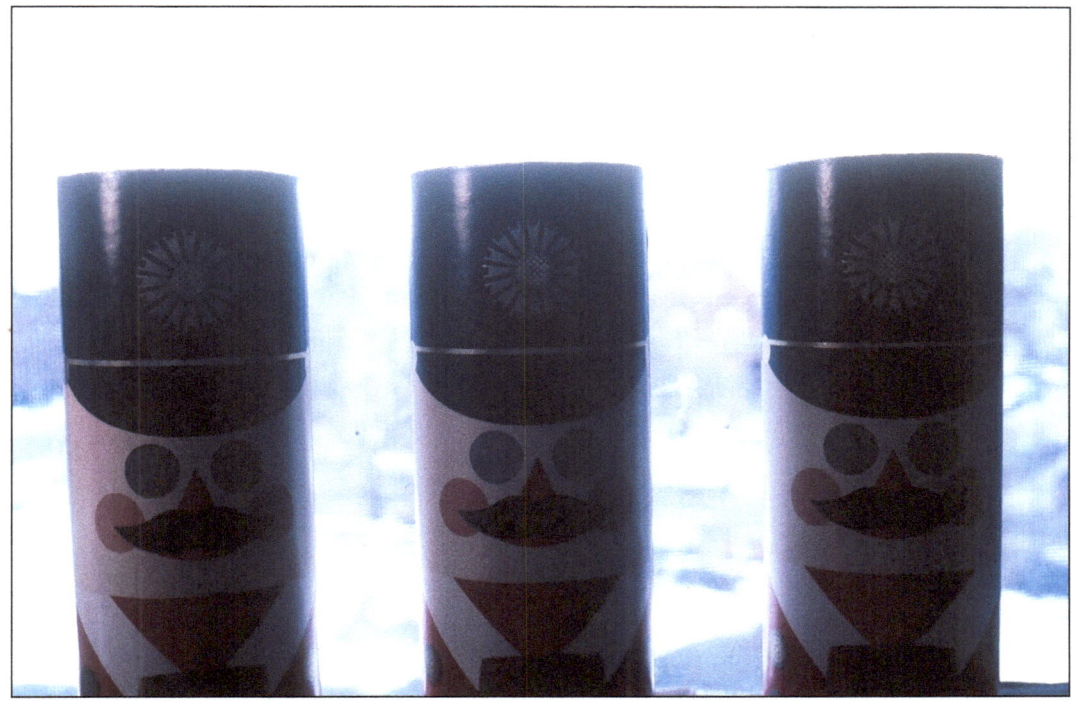

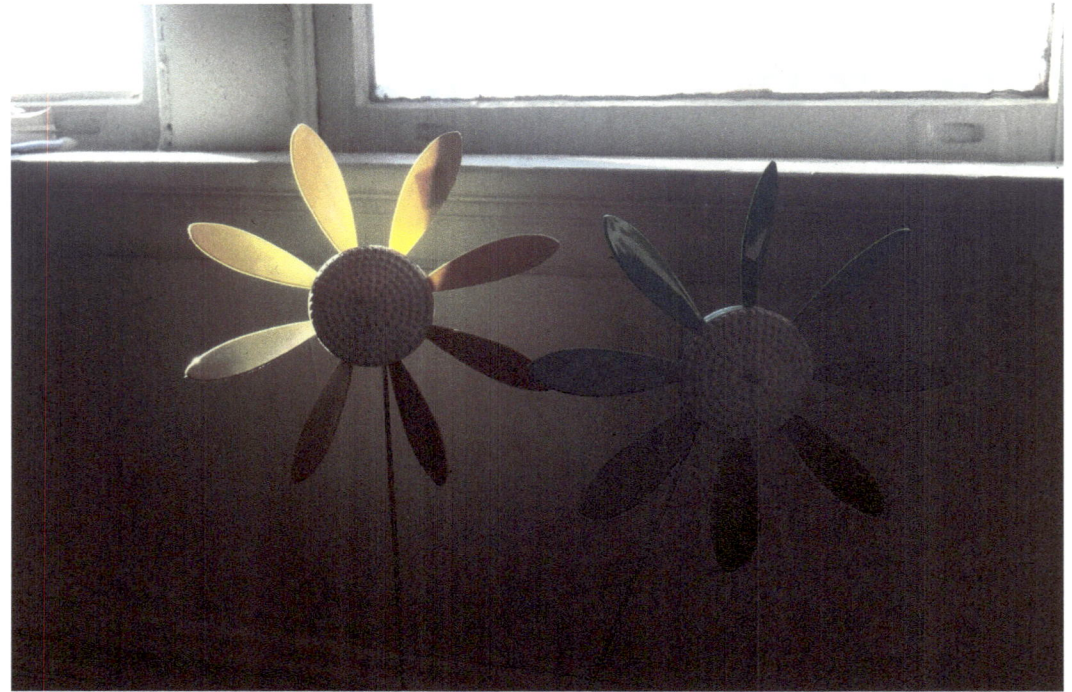

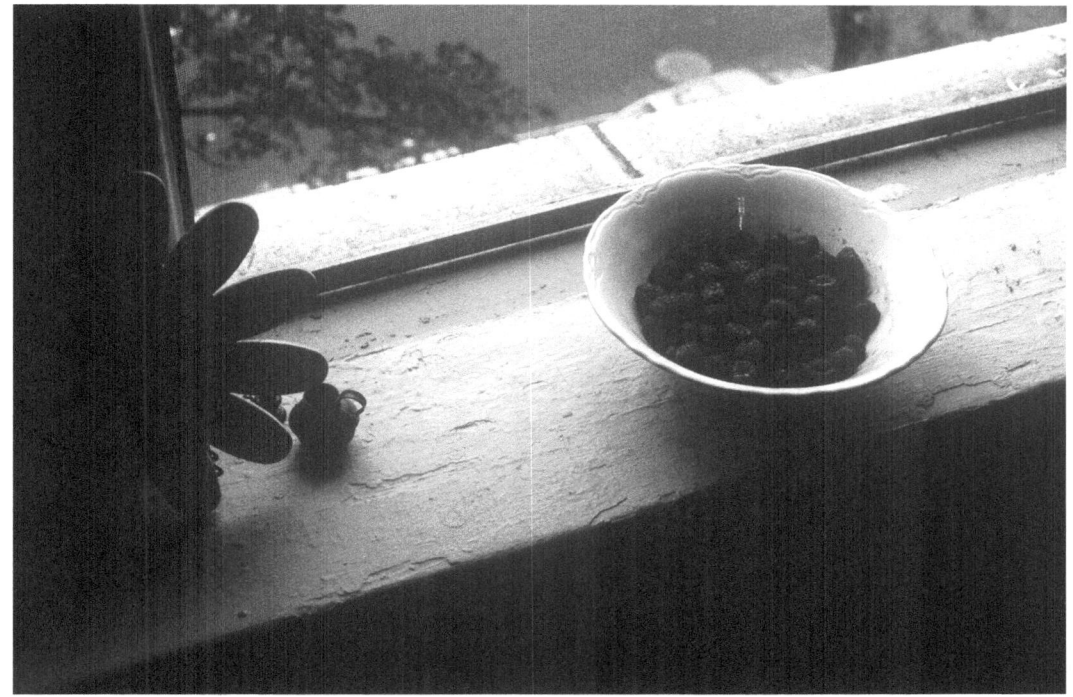

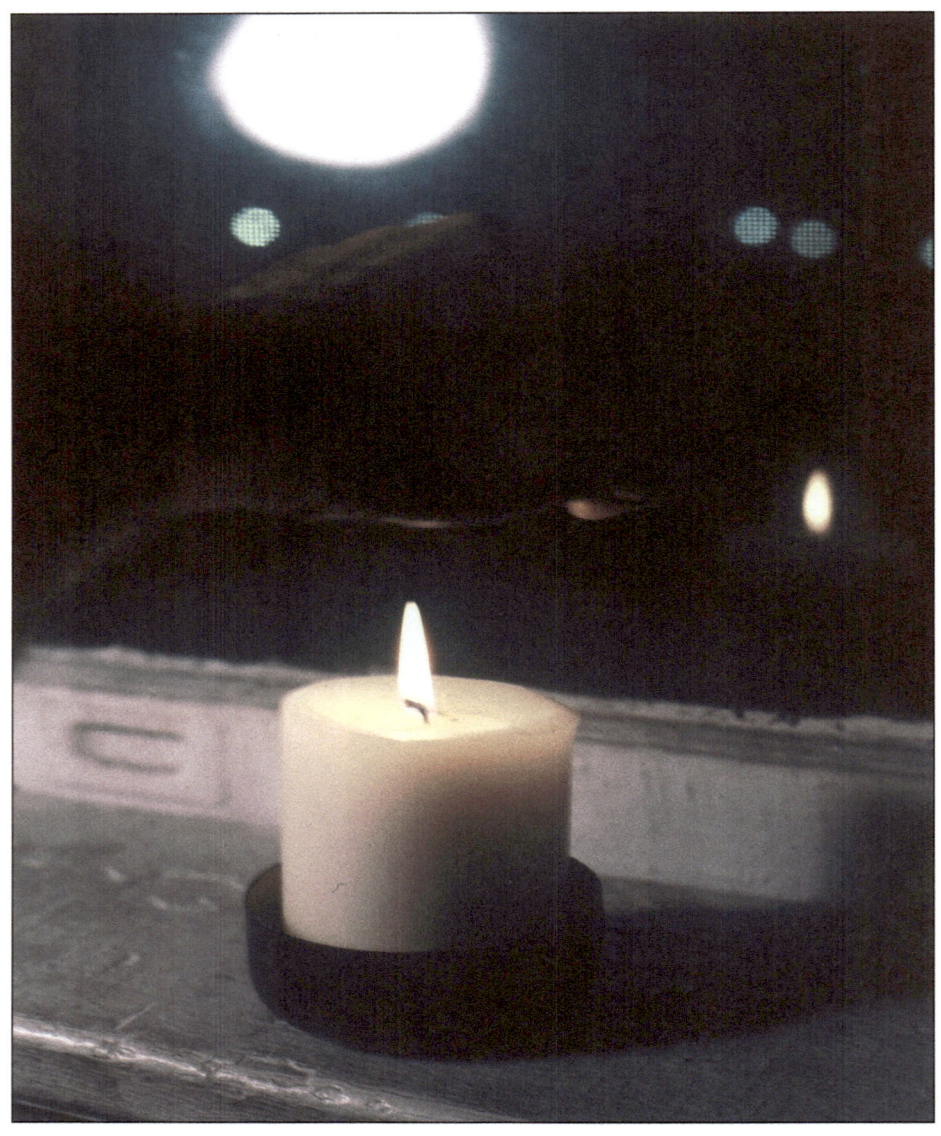

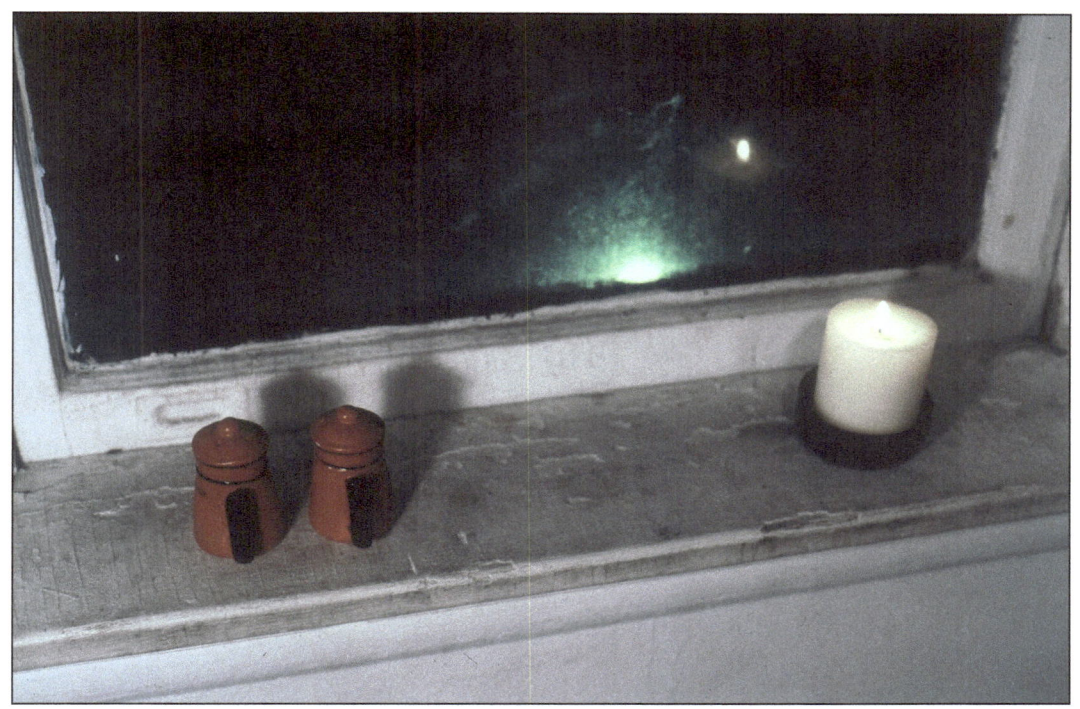

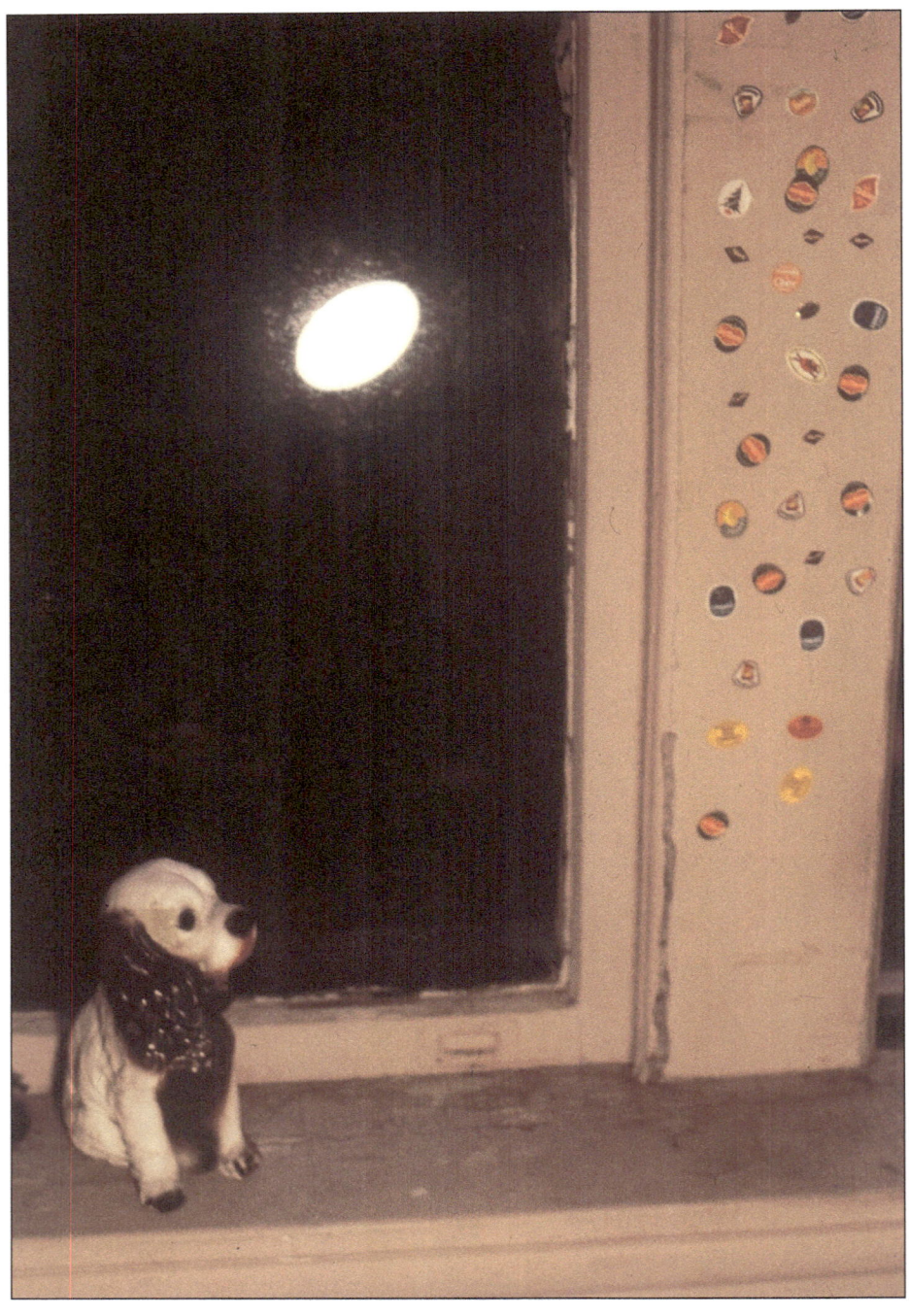

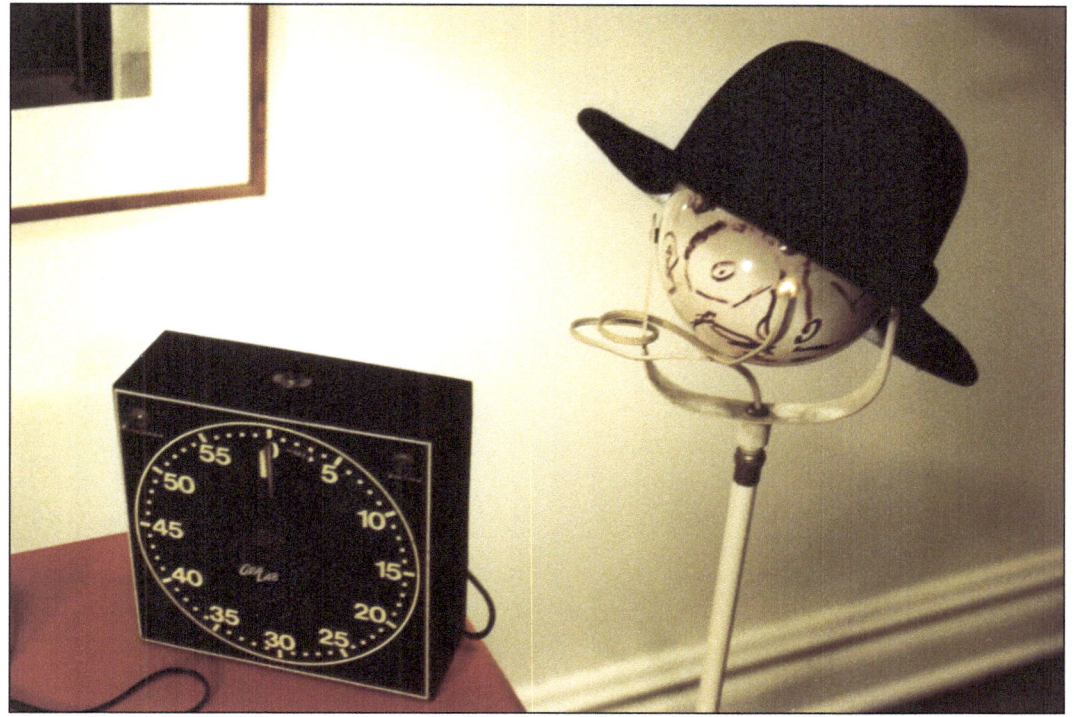

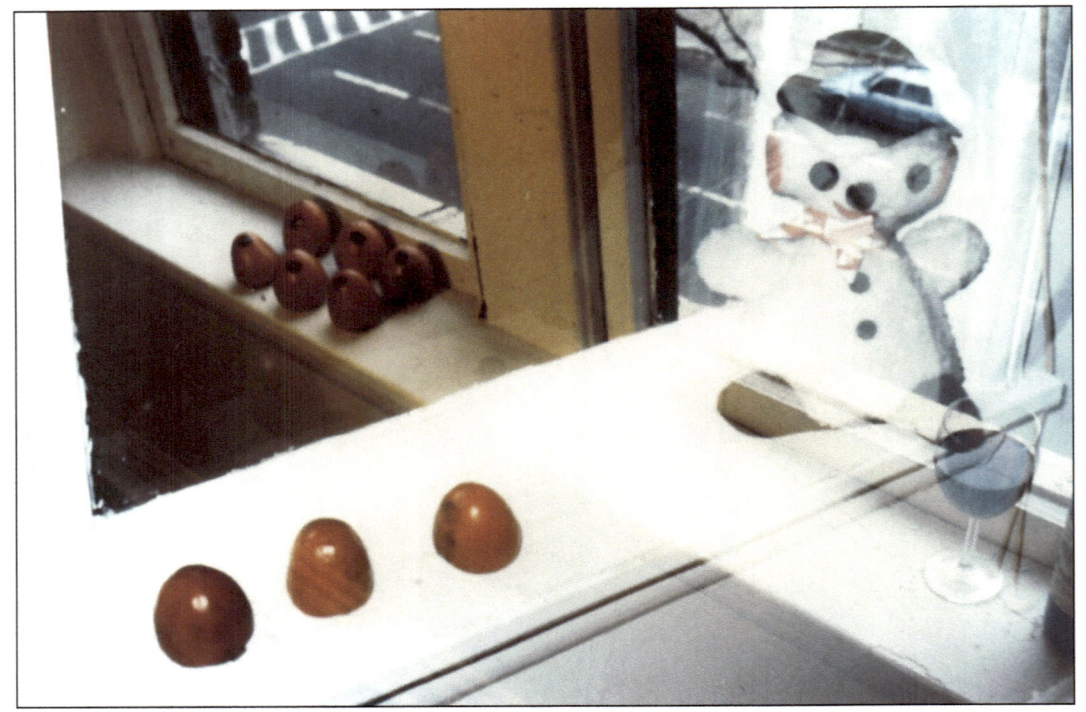

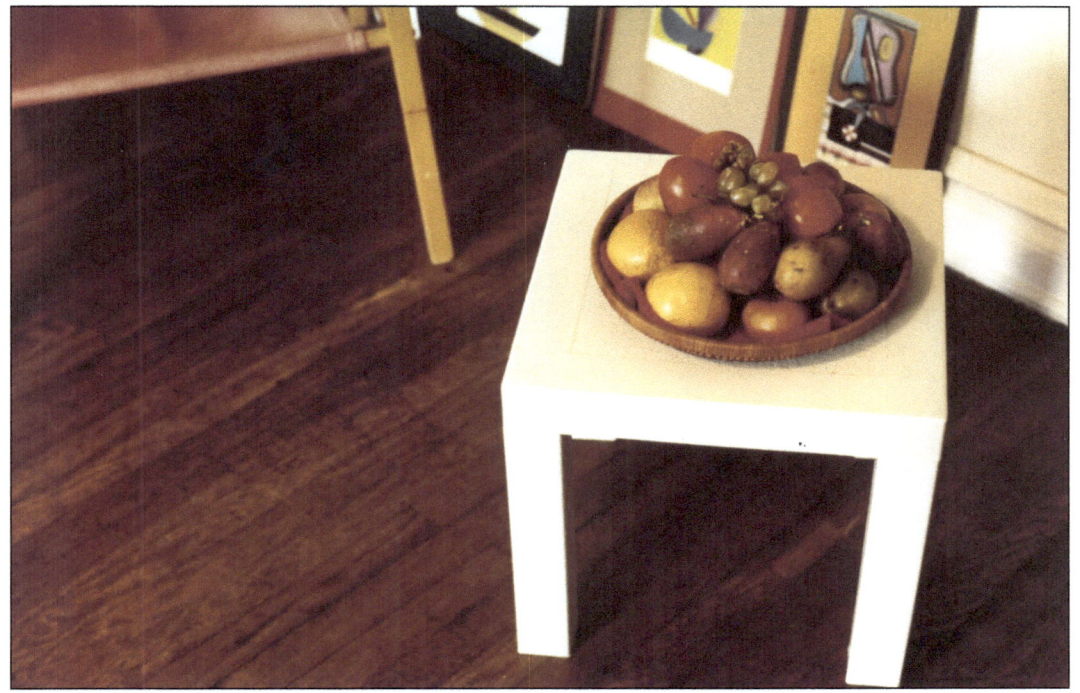

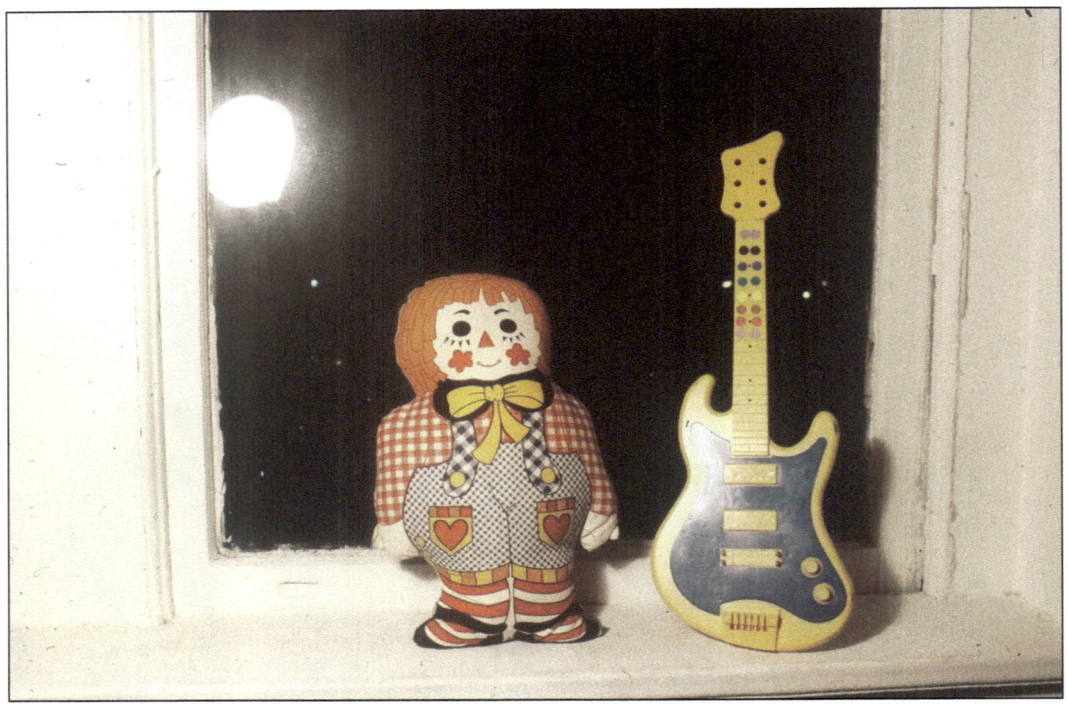

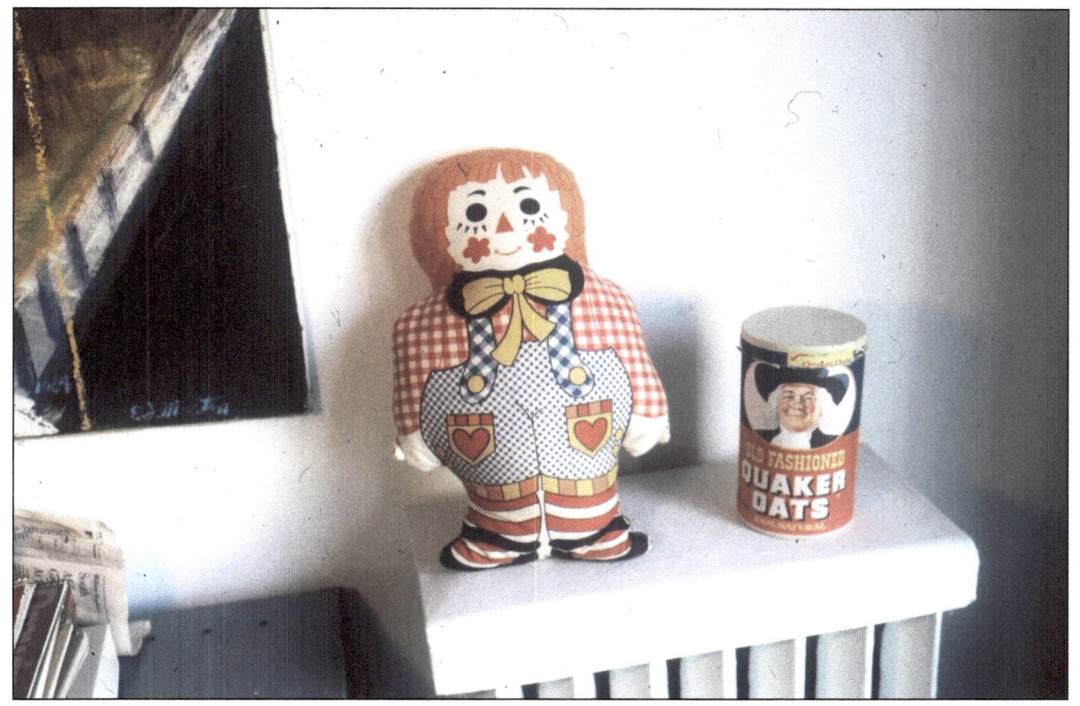

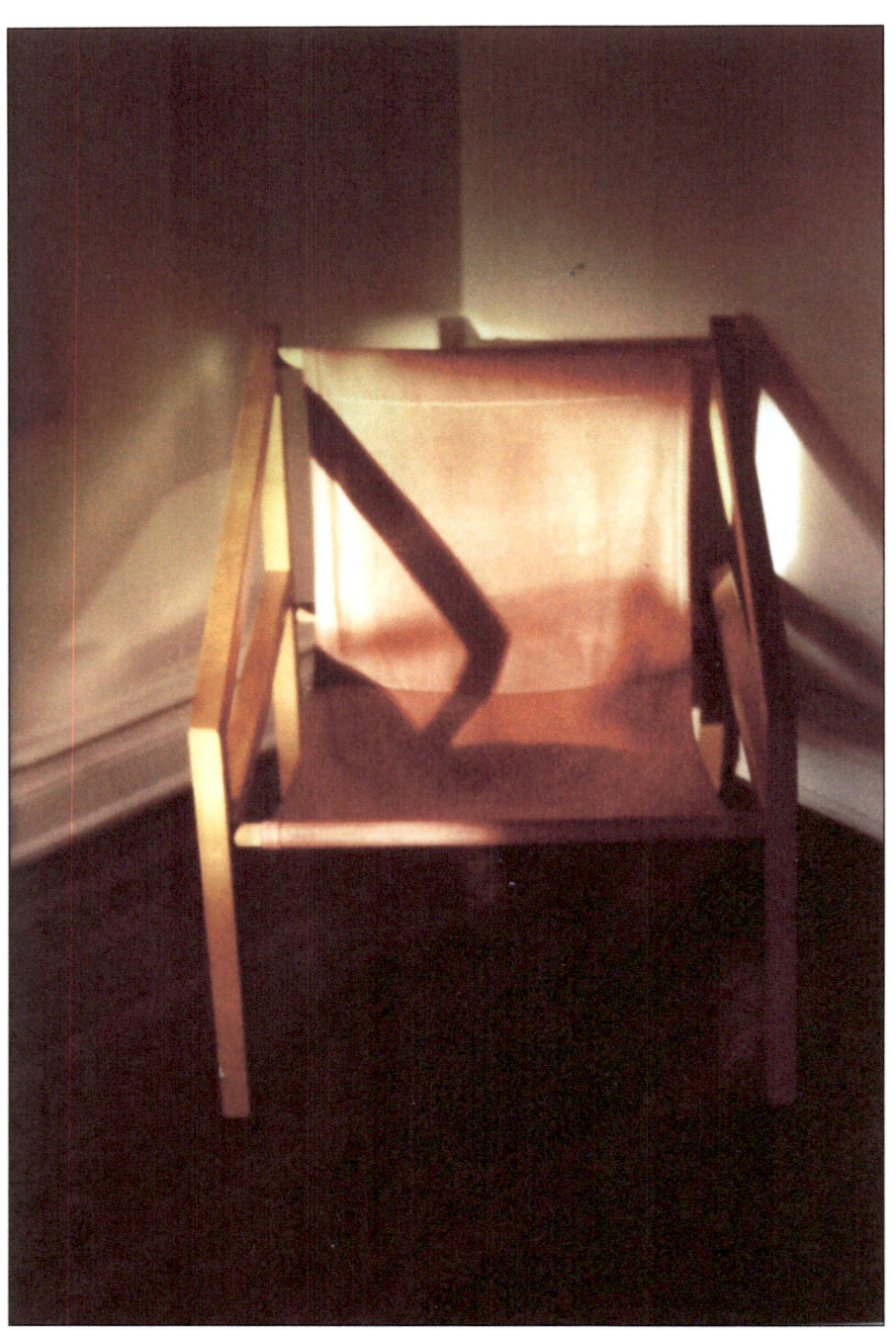

Eugene's Chair, 1981

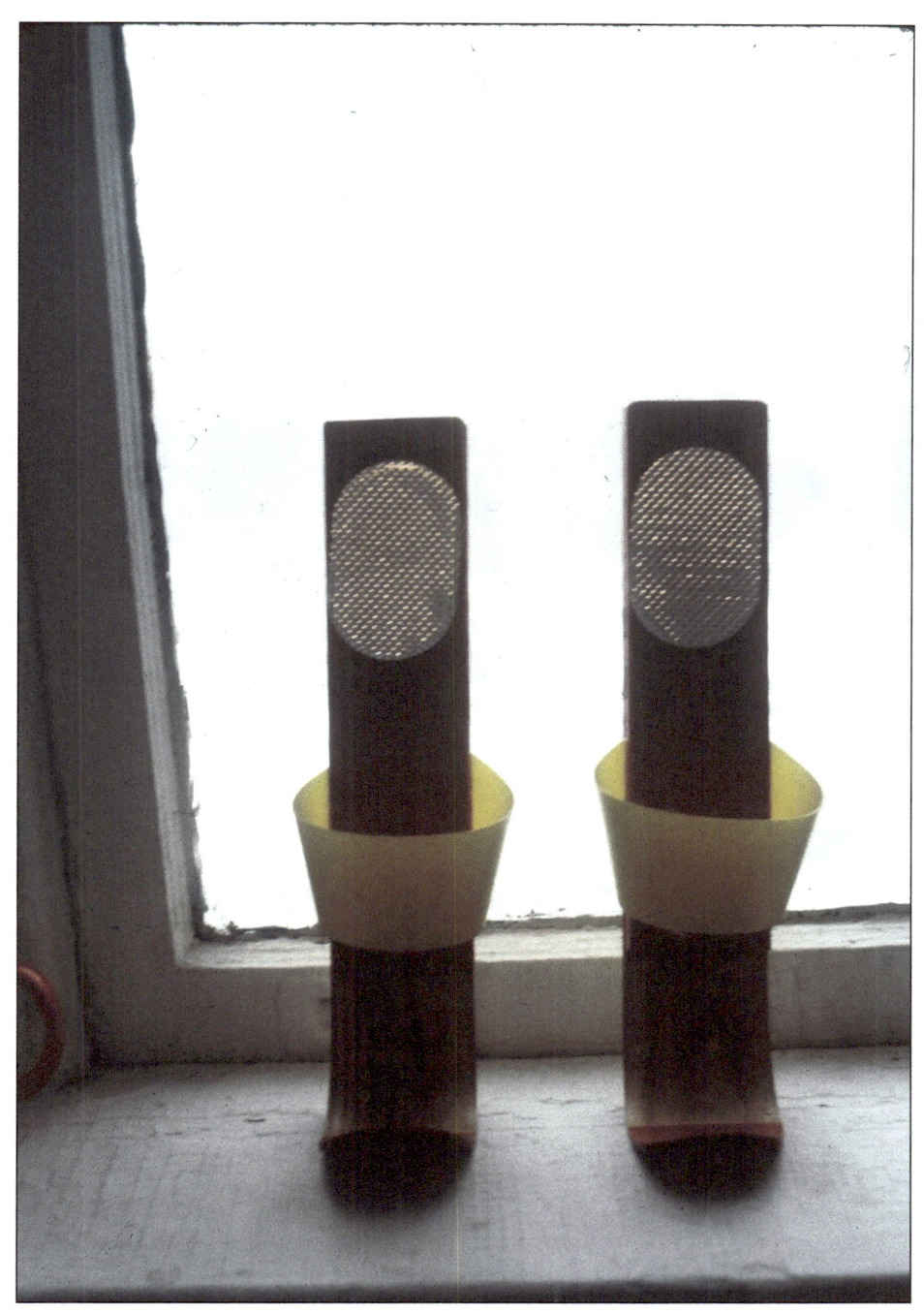

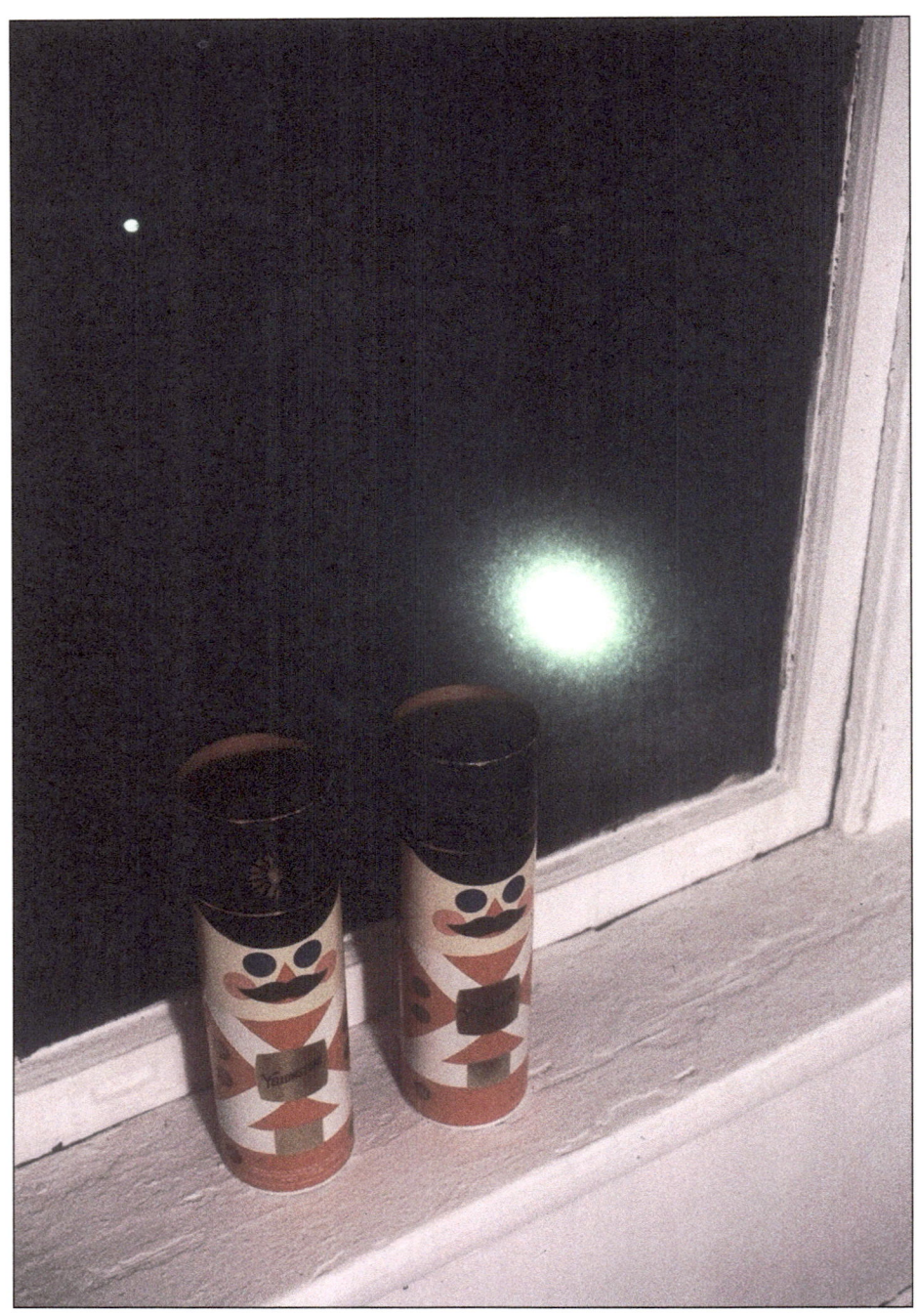

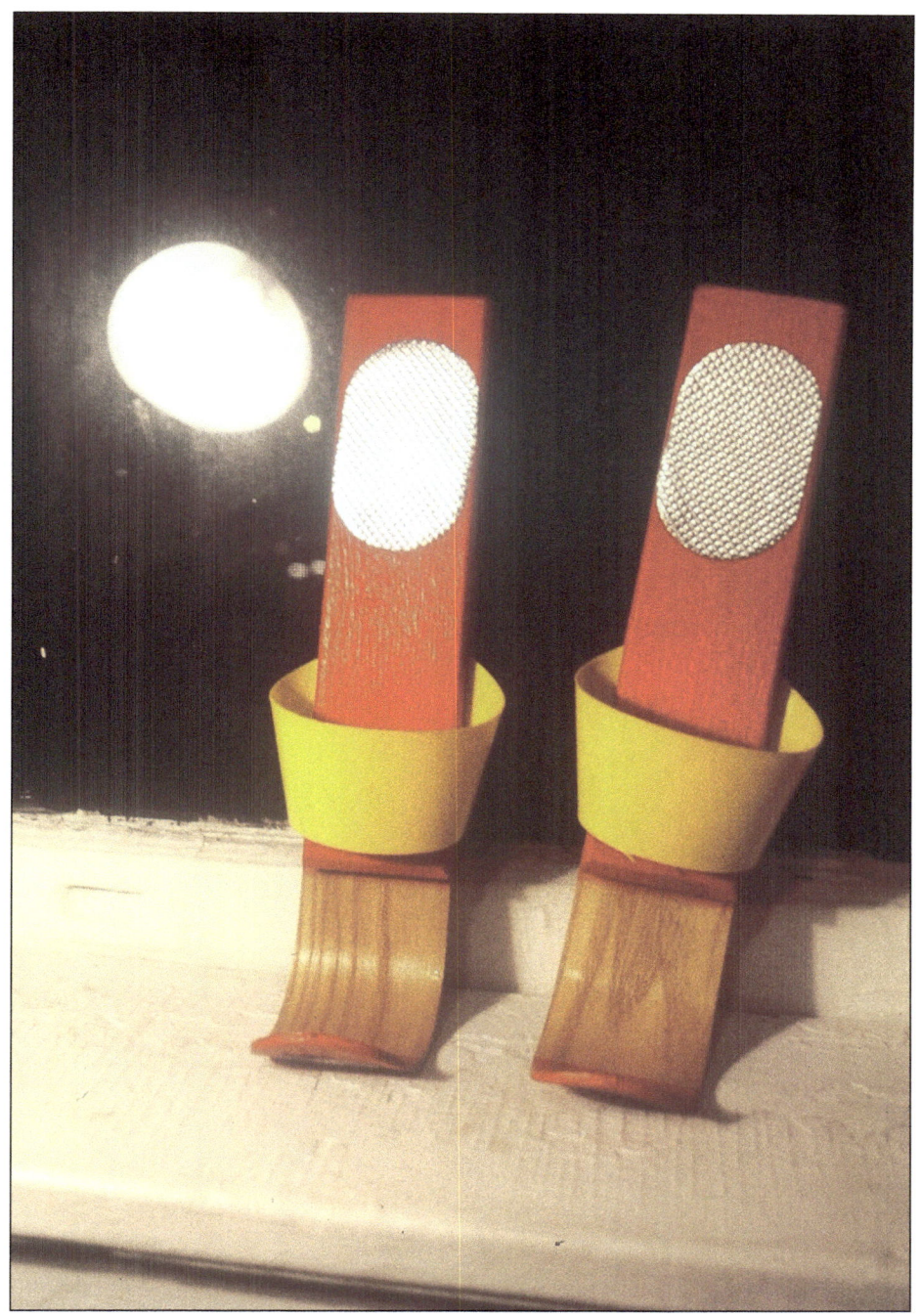

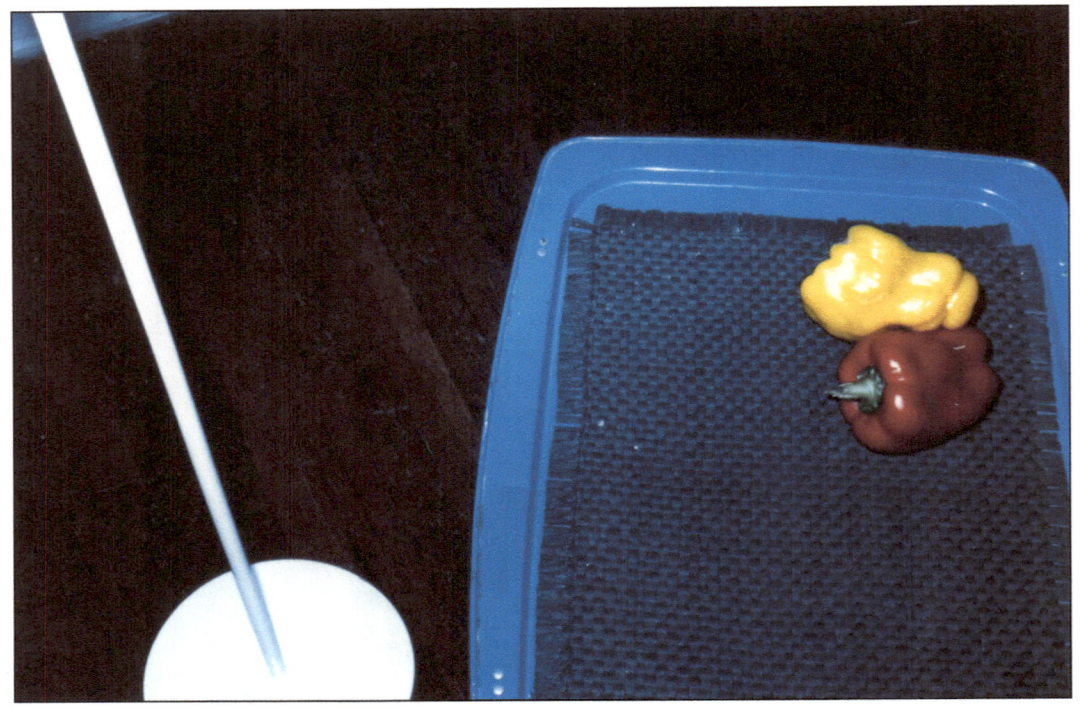

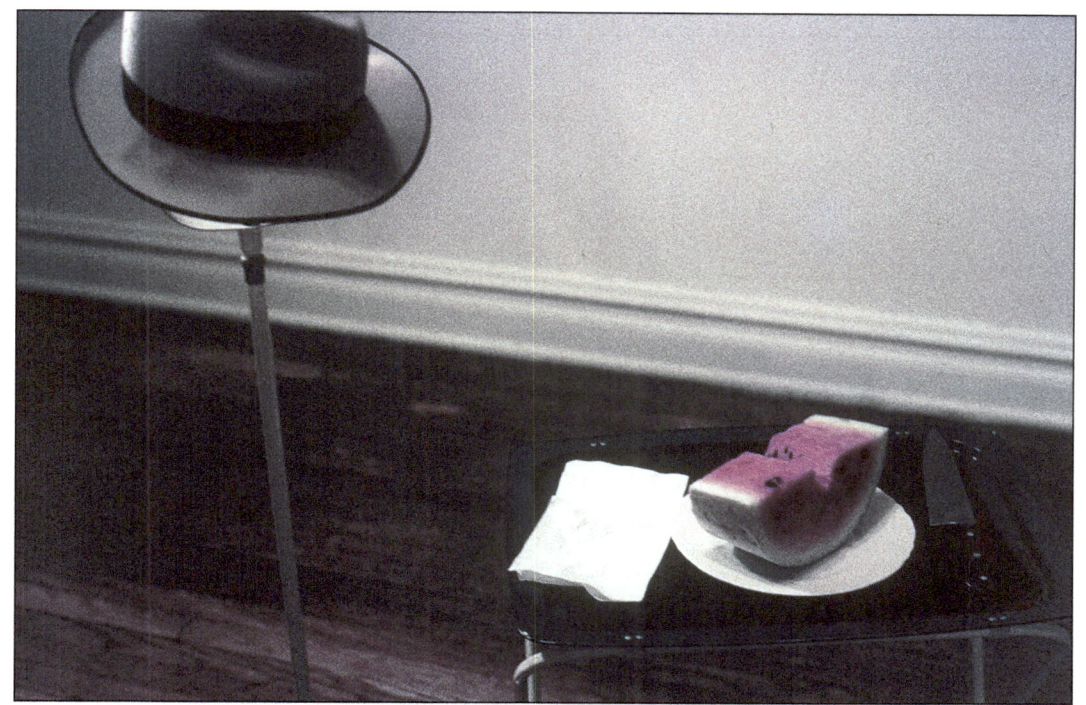

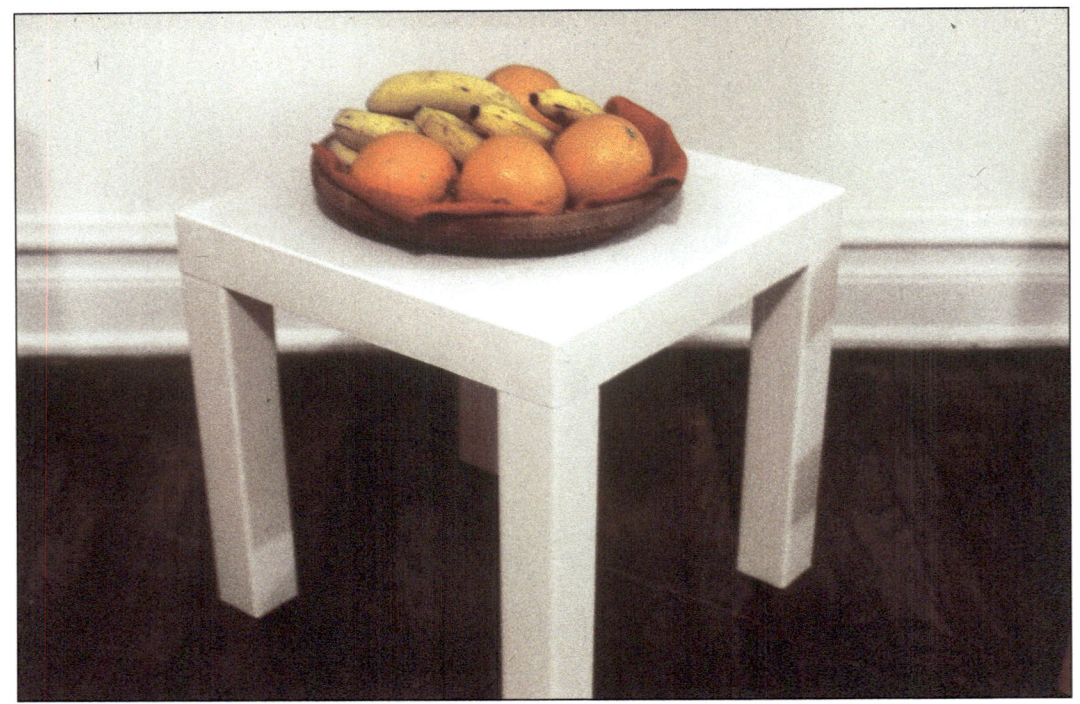

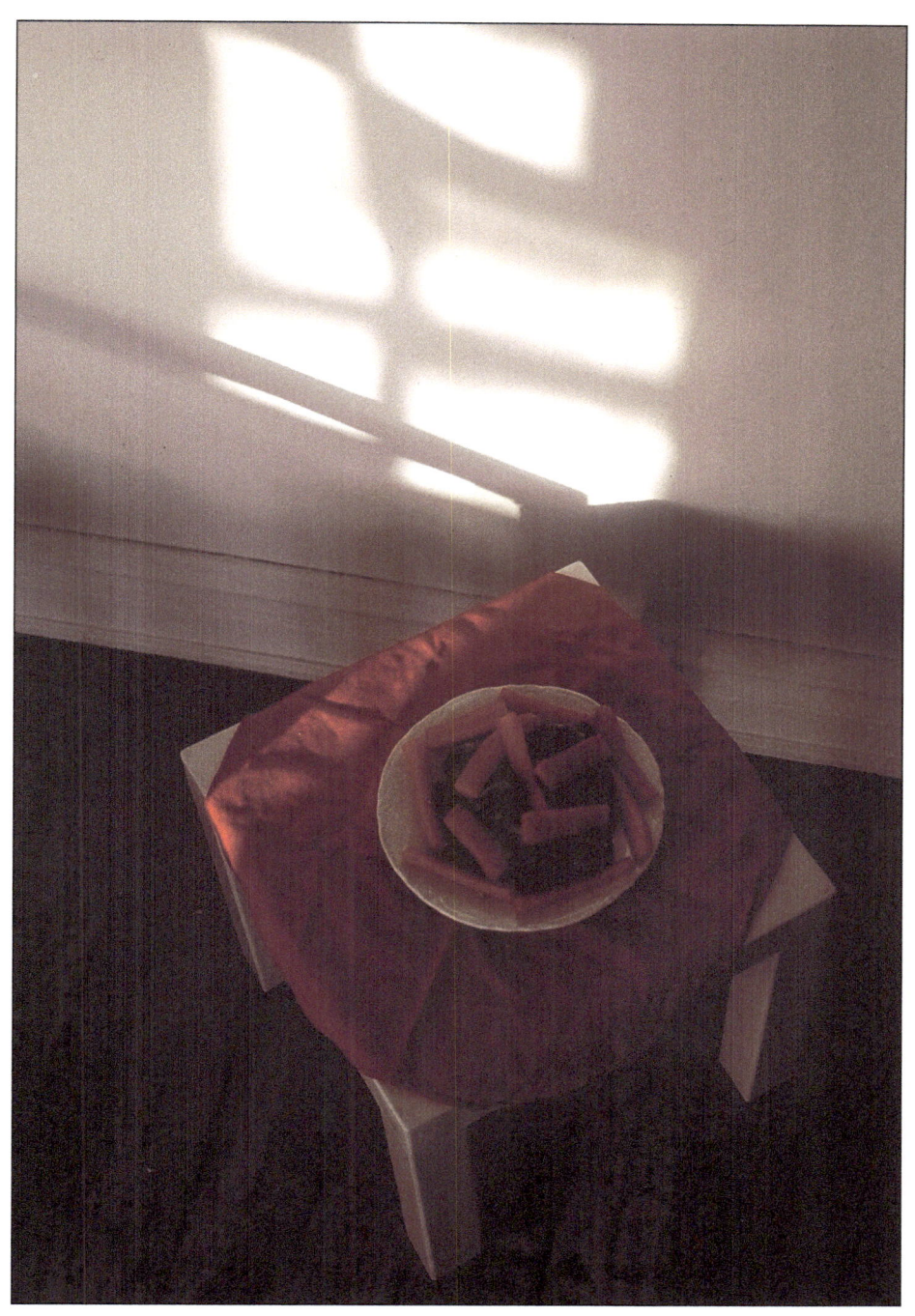

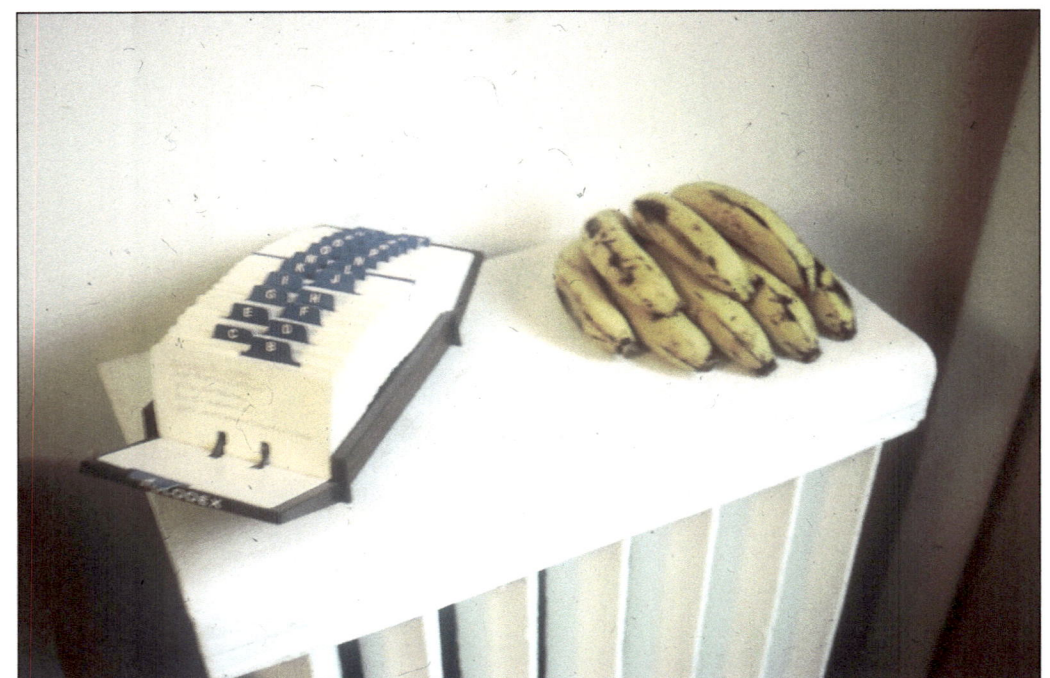

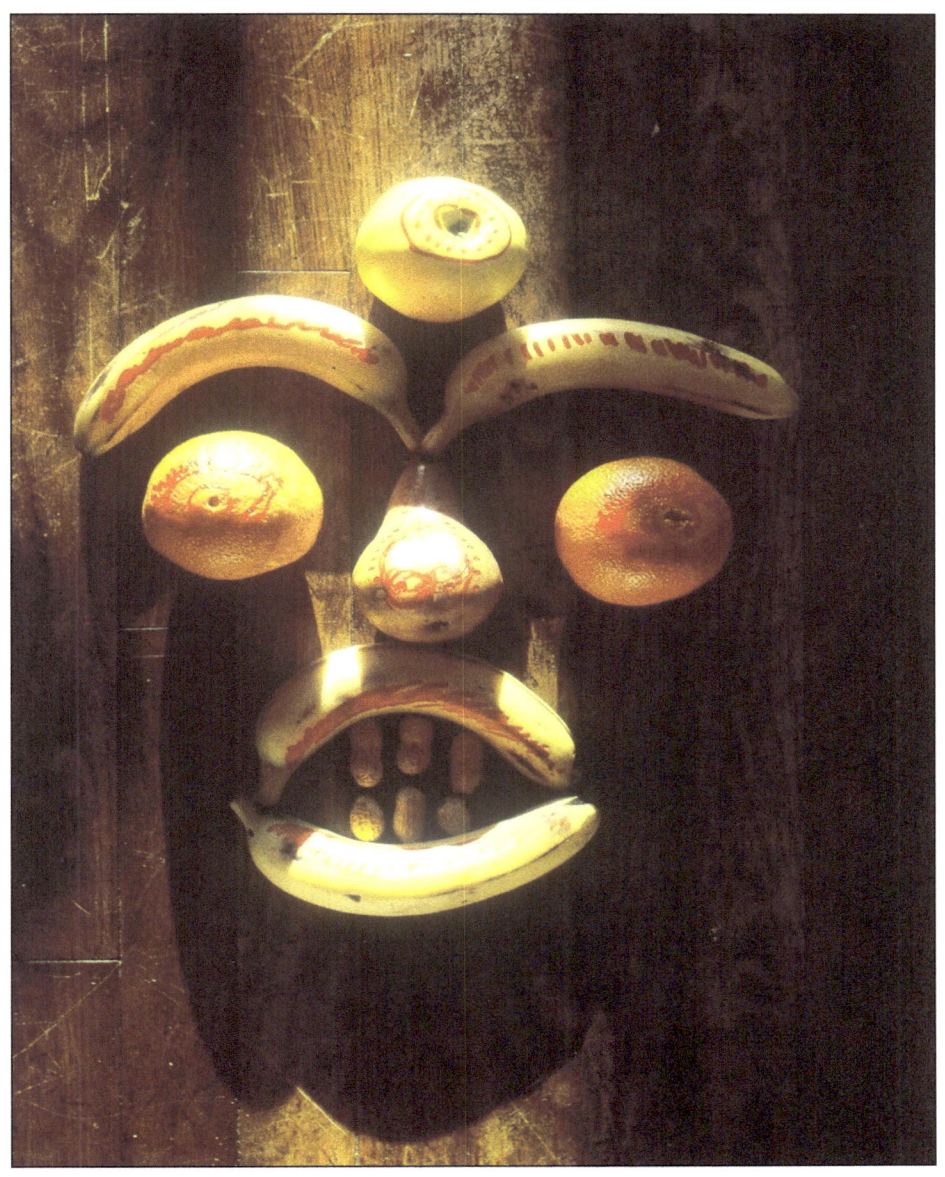

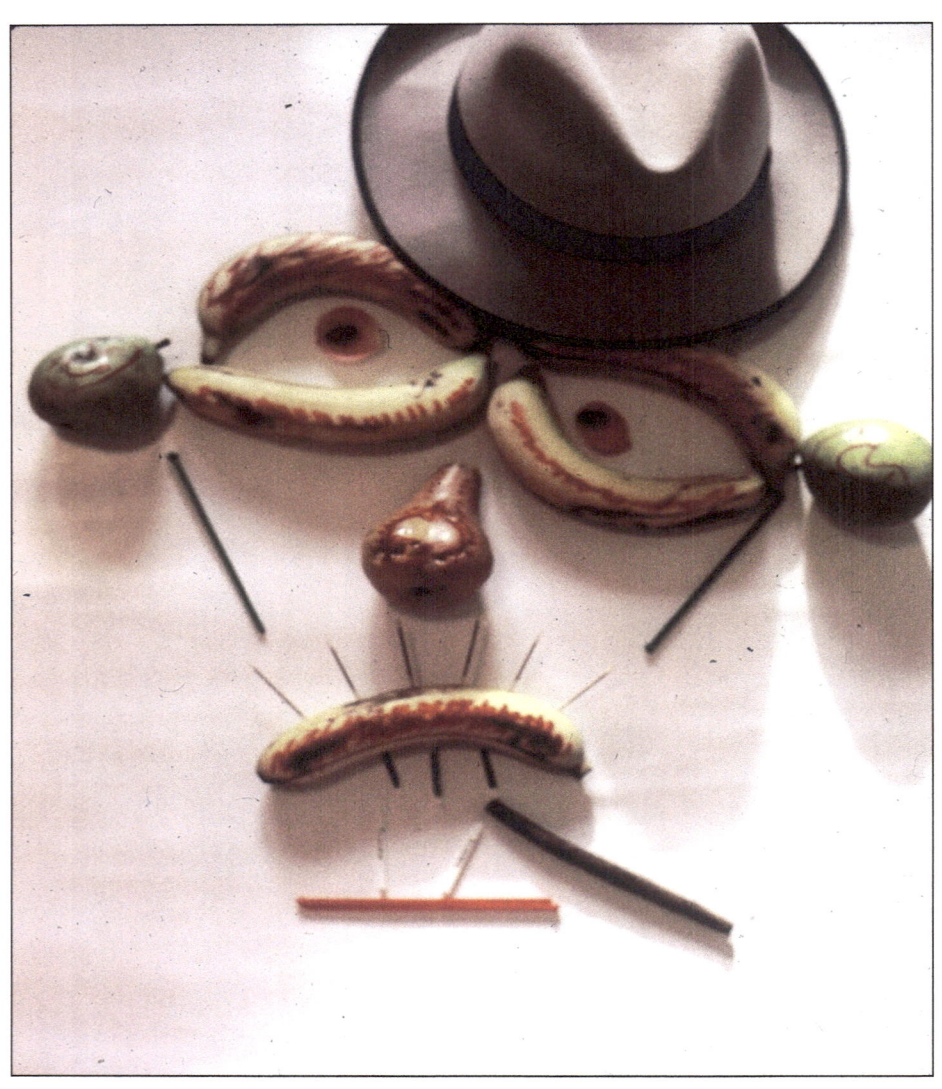

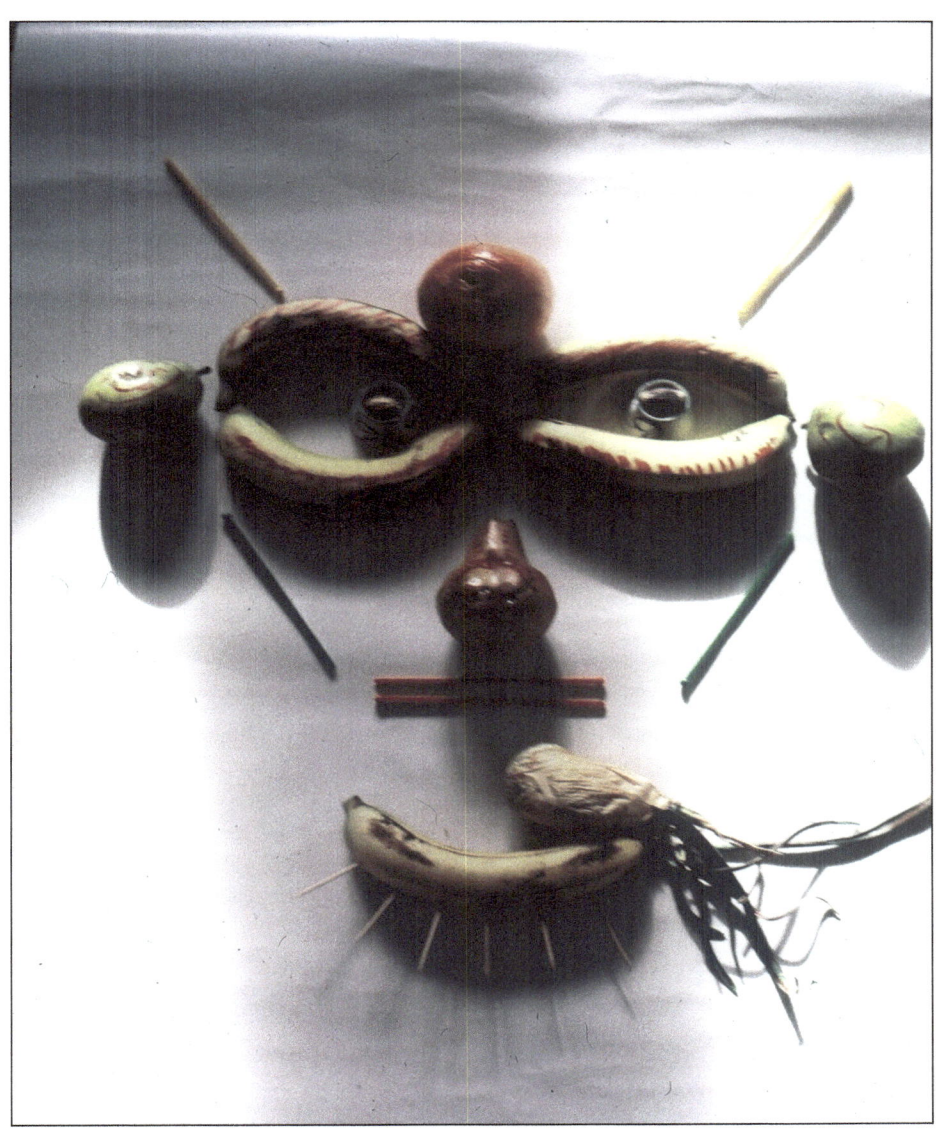

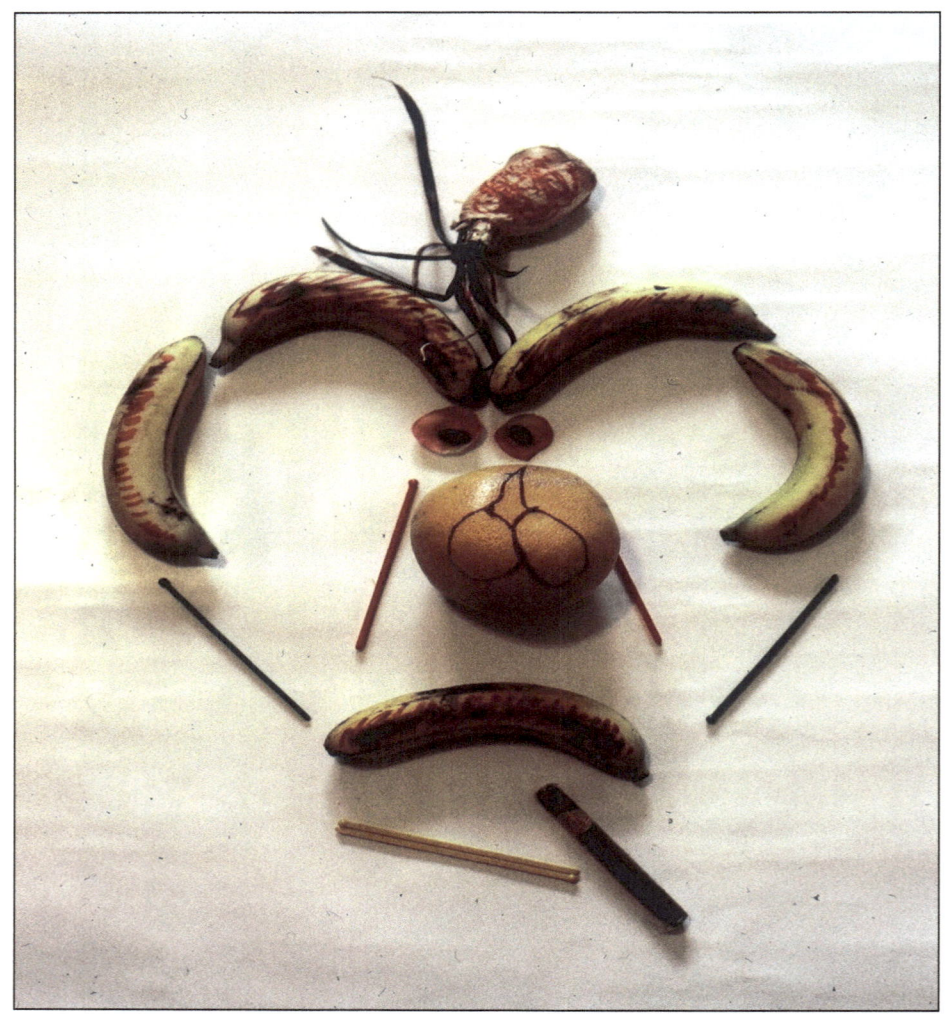

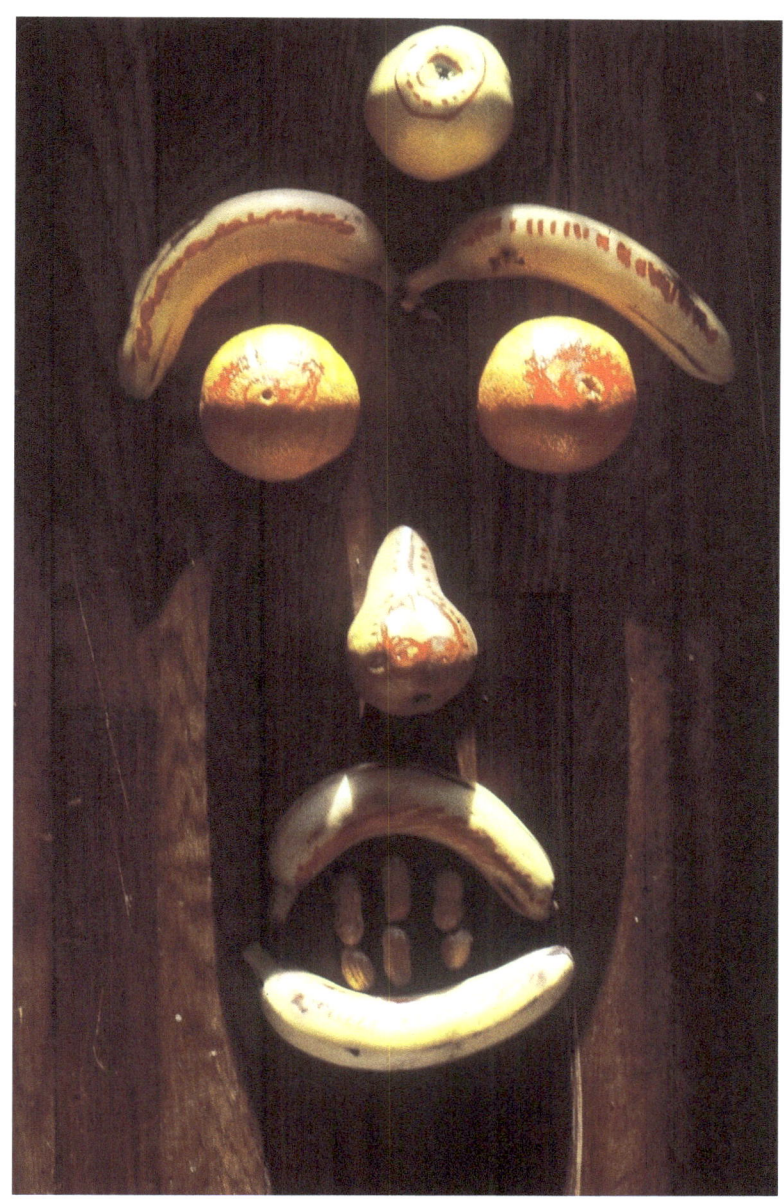

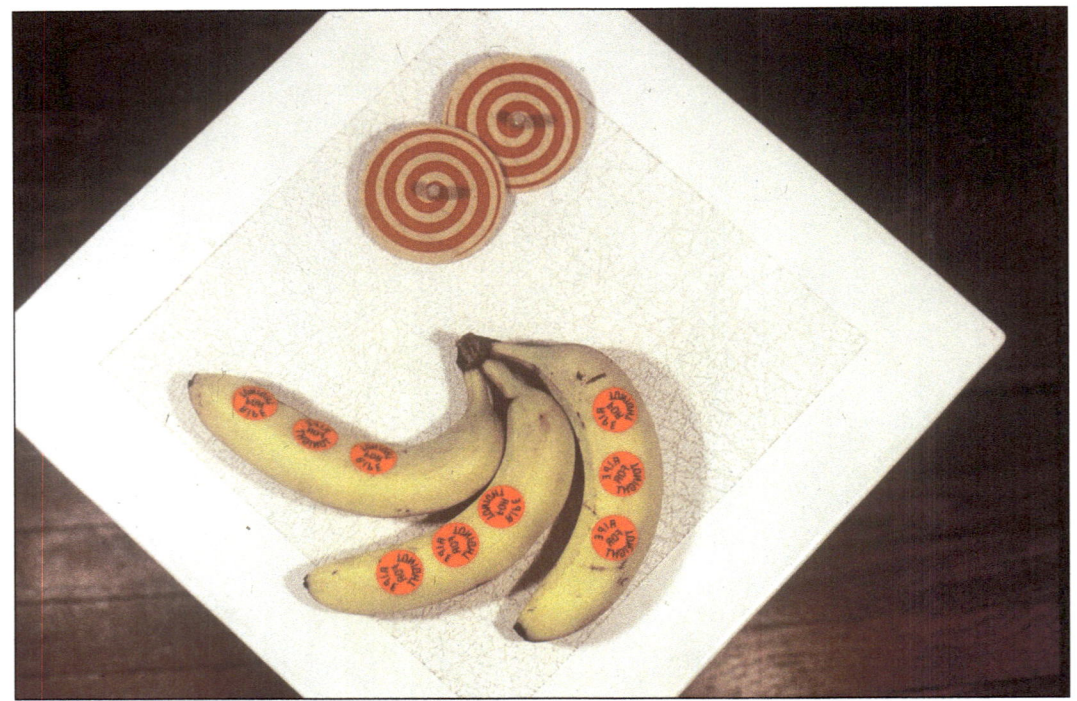

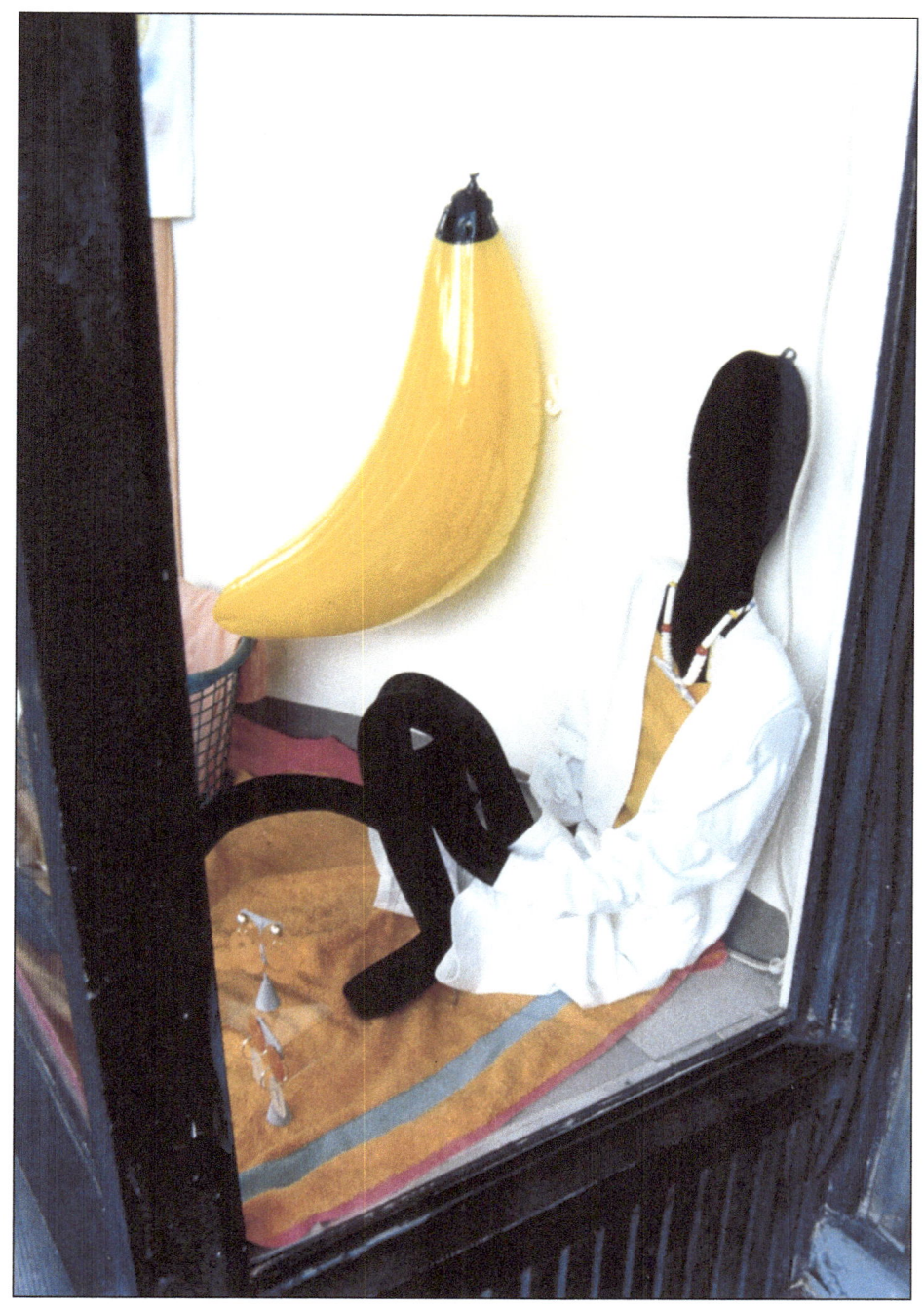

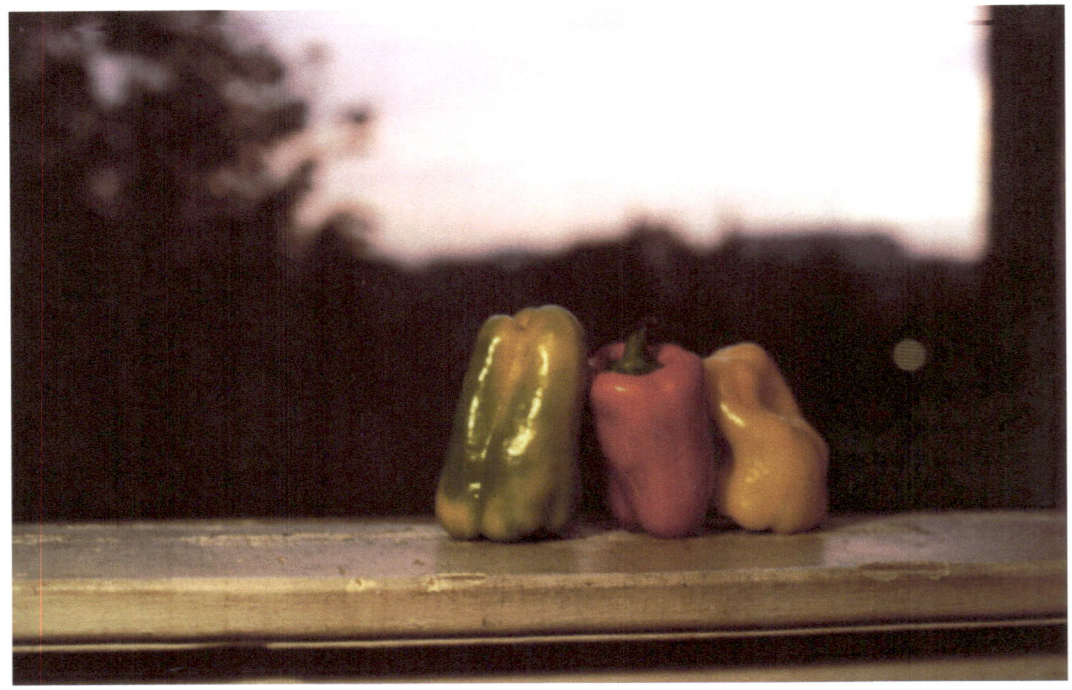